Heaven and Hell

Alex Buchanan

Sovereign World

Sovereign World Ltd
PO Box 777
Tonbridge
Kent TN11 9XT
England

ISBN 1 85240 154 0

Typeset by CRB Associates, Lenwade, Norwich
Printed in England by Clays Ltd, St. Ives plc

Contents

Foreword

I regard it both an honour and a responsibility to commend Alex Buchanan's book to you. I have known Alex and Peggy Buchanan for about ten years, having met them first at Spring Harvest. My wife Louise and I have found them among the exceedingly rare people we could turn to when we ourselves needed pastoral help. I cannot stress enough how much we respect them. Few, if any, have suffered more. Yet they never complain but rather spend much of their time listening to the complaints of others who seek their wise and (often) prophetic counsel.

But why do I regard this Foreword as a responsibility? Because Alex has focused on the most crucial matter that could possibly exist – where will we spend Eternity? In a day in which the Christian faith is often seen as 'what will it do for me in this life?' rather than (1) the real reason God sent His Son to die on the cross and (2) why one should really become a Christian, this book brings us back to the true essentials. The apostle Paul would not agree with those who say, 'If there were no Heaven or no Hell I would still be a Christian'. No! Says Paul, *If only for this life we have hope in Christ, we are to be pitied more than all men'* (1 Corinthians 15:19).

The message of this book must be recovered if the Church is to be restored to its true glory. The 'Toronto Blessing' (which is of God) must lead those who have experienced it to the burden of this book if they are to mature and truly begin to shake the nations. I recommend that every Christian on both sides of the Atlantic will read this book – to its very end. It is also relevant at the present time since the theory of annihilation – once the exclusive belief of the cults – has sadly crept into the Church. Alex has no time for this deceptive teaching which is but a rationale for what the unbeliever already hopes is true.

Alex writes as an exhorter and prophet not as a theologian or academic. His purpose is to 'enthuse' us to look forward to Heaven and to warn of God's Hell. He achieves his goal admirably and I myself have been stirred by reading it – and have also learned from it. Those who know Alex love his inimitable style and will smile, sometimes laugh, as they read.

But what I like most about this book is that Alex never apologises for God or the Bible. Few books written nowadays contain so much Scripture. He lets Scripture speak for itself, and I love the way he uses the Old Testament as well as the New. He does not try to solve all the eschatological (doctrine of 'last things') problems his book raises but gently lets us know where he stands on certain controversial issues.

This book gives us a consciousness of Heaven. Alex is describing my future home. Is it yours? If not, read this book with fear and trembling. If it describes your future home also, get copies of this book for your non-Christian friends; it is the kindest thing you will ever do for them.

It describes Alex's future home too. I could not help but think about Alex and Peggy as I read. Those who know them will think the same thing: one day Alex's paralysed face and Peggy's paralysed body will be made new. There will be no wheelchairs in Heaven. They look forward to a place where God will wipe away all tears, and suffering will be no more. And best of all, Heaven can be anybody's home – if one will take seriously this book's message.

Dr R.T. Kendall
Westminster Chapel
London
March 1994

Preface

This book is intended to enthuse and encourage more than to teach in an academic way. To urge God's people to get on with the job more than to fill the head with facts. To make us stop and think more than to toss theology to and fro. To stir up, more than to give an accurate answer to every question. I am more concerned to enthuse the church about these truths than to inform; more anxious to envision than to examine all the arguments. I write for the plain person, and I want to help the church to feel passionately about these two neglected doctrines, rather than to engage in verbal gymnastics. So I will continue to use the terms Heaven and Hell generally because the words at least are fairly well understood by today's Christians. There are many things which I do not know. There are some things which I do not completely understand. However, I want to share some of the things which I do feel strongly about. There are many books on such things as the Second Coming and the Resurrection, so my writings on these subjects will not be exhaustive.

There are many dangers confronting those who write about the hereafter. One of them is that of allowing imagination to run riot, although imagination is God-given, and is useful as long as it does not run counter to Scripture. Another danger is that of being over-absorbed in Heaven and Hell to the detriment of preaching the Gospel, and establishing the church down here. The jibe 'so heavenly minded that we are no earthly use' is a cheap one, but does contain an element of truth. However, I say that if we are not heavenly minded, then we cannot be of much earthly use! Yet another danger is that of taking every word literally when it is not justified. For example *Let the rivers clap their hands, let the mountains sing together for joy'* (Psalm 98:8). To take this literally is ridiculous. It is a poetic outburst from the heart of a man who is praising God, and inviting all and sundry to do the same. When John saw into Heaven, he mentions some creatures who had strange characteristics – *Also before the throne there was what looked like a sea of glass, clear as crystal. In the centre, around the throne, were four living creatures, and they were **covered with eyes, in front and behind*** (Revelation 4:6). I believe that this is not literal, but illustrative of the fact that they miss nothing.

I am aware that the terms we use such as Heaven and Hell need some explanation. The terms Heaven and heavenlies in Scripture can denote the starry and the cloudy Heavens; the heavenlies in which principalities and powers operate; and Heaven which is God's home. And even this latter is not the final Heaven. The word Hell is a bit misleading too. Scripture speaks of Sheol and Hades, the place of departed spirits. It is also speaks of The lake of Fire as being the final Hell. I deal with these terms more fully later in the book.

I base everything I write on the Bible, or at least, my understanding of it. I believe implicitly in the veracity of Scripture, and that it is the true Word of God. In it God makes direct mention of Heaven and Hell, but the details are not always clear. However, we can legitimately deduce or infer some things from Scripture. For example, Heaven is described as a place where there is no fear. It is not difficult to picture such a place if we think about our earth, and all the violence, robbery, wars, and then imagine it without such things. As long as our inferences do not contradict the Bible, we are on safe ground.

I want to write about both Heaven and Hell in this book because I wanted to include the joyful with the solemn; to show that there is a Heaven to be gained as well as a Hell to be shunned. We cannot have a balanced understanding of one without the other. I rejoice to write about Heaven, but I never wanted to write about Hell. I still struggle with a reluctance to deal with the subject, but I write because it is a neglected doctrine, even amongst evangelicals.

Jesus preached about Heaven and Hell

Because He believed in these basic truths, He preached them wherever He went. He found many who were indifferent to their eternal future, and He found those like the Sadducees who simply scorned the whole idea of eternal existence. This is mirrored today. I rarely hear anyone preach on Heaven; most Christians seem to hold the view that we must get on with work down here, and as for Heaven – 'it will be alright on the night'. Still fewer people preach about Hell. Some do believe in it, but they prefer to speak of annihilation rather than eternal punishment. I note with dismay the re-emergence in the church of the theory of annihilation; one which I regard as heresy, and one which I totally reject. We should preach about Hell because Jesus preached about it, and about Heaven for the same reason. If we need another reason for preaching about these vital truths, we find it in this simple statement – it is plainly in Scripture. If we are to be His true followers, we must preach both with equal zeal. If He regarded it as vital to do so, then so must we. People still reject these doctrines today, but, just as He persevered in preaching them, so must we. He never preached anything which He did not believe. He preached as a sign of His great love and concern for mankind. His attitude is well illustrated in Scripture – *The Lord is not slow in keeping his promise, as some understand slowness. He is patient with you, not wanting anyone to perish, but everyone to come to repentance* (2 Peter 3:9).

Beliefs which are only held in the mind but never spoken

9

out, are not beliefs at all. The urgency with which Jesus preached His beliefs showed His conviction as to their reality. He preached the Gospel, which declares God's intolerance of evil; His anger because of it; His punishment of it, and His dogmatism. He is opposed to the world's easy going, 'anything goes' philosophy, therefore, we must oppose it. God demands that we preach His truths with passion. I rejoice greatly in the truth of Heaven, but I wish that I could weep over the horrors of Hell more than I do, but I try.

The deciding factor as to where we spend eternity is our obedience to Jesus, and His Word. True Gospel preaching will make this plain, and it will include the truths of Heaven and Hell. Faulty Gospel preaching is likely to produce faulty Christians i.e. those who profess to be saved, but who may not really be saved at all. Those who preach only the love of God and not His anger, tremble on the edge of blasphemy. They misrepresent Him if they neglect to preach His holiness and judgement too.

Life here is brief, and we must use our time well and be a benefit to the world around us, but is this life all we are intended to experience? Not according to Scripture. Man was made in the Image of God; eternal; made for eternity. So then, we must have an eternal perspective, and realise that our life down here is mainly a preparation for eternity. Satan will use anything to deflect man's attention from his eternal destiny. His methods include fear of the unknown, fear of ridicule, and absorption with the here and now. He does not mind being caricatured, for this tends to make him an unreal being in the minds of some. It is up to us to defeat his objective by directing our attention again to these real, basic doctrines of our faith, and then to preach and teach with all the power of the Holy Spirit. May we get on and do so!

One final point – I write quite briefly about some important doctrines such as the Resurrection, and the Second Coming. My reason for this brevity is that there are so many good and scholarly books written about them. If my readers want to have a more detailed study on these subjects, I would urge them to find these other books. I also write only briefly about the Millenium. My reason for that is that there are so many points of view that I fear lest I get so absorbed in them that I fail in my major objective – to enthuse us about Heaven, to warn us about Hell, and to encourage us to preach the Gospel.

Alex Buchanan
York 1994

SECTION 1:

Heaven

Chapter 1

Heaven – a Neglected Truth

Phroneo
φρονεω
(its affections in
KJV)
cf use in Rom 8:5
Phil 3:16
:19

Few Christians think about Heaven but every Christian ought to do so, for God demands it. Consider this Scripture – *Since, then, you have been raised with Christ,* **set your hearts** *on things above, where Christ is seated at the right hand of God.* **Set your minds** *on things above, not on earthly things'* (Colossians 3:1–2). 'Setting the mind' is a strong term. It is the same thing which Jesus did when He *resolutely set out for Jerusalem* (Luke 9:51). Jesus **set** His face. Nothing was going to stop Him from obeying the prompting of the Holy Spirit. It was time to go towards Calvary, and His love for His Father and His desire to accomplish our salvation was so strong, that He allowed nothing to stand in His way. This is the same determination that God requires of us as we do what He says in the above Scripture – **Set your minds** *on things above,* to think constantly about Heaven, His Home, and ours. God has laid down the injunction to consider Heaven but many Christians disobey Him, and yet profess to love Him! We should obey this Scripture as much as any other commandment, and church leaders must be faithful in preaching these two great doctrines of our faith: Heaven and Hell.

It is an insult to Jesus to neglect Heaven. Just think – He has personally prepared a place for you in His home. What a staggering thought that God the Son has been getting your home ready for you. If He has gone to such trouble to make it possible for us to live in Heaven forever, how can we neglect to think of it, anticipate it, and speak about it to one another? Remember what He has so tenderly said – *And if I go and prepare a place for you, I will come back and take you to be with me that you also may be where I am* (John 14:3). God could have got the angels to prepare a place for us in Heaven, after all, they are His servants. He could have given them a general instruction to let us in when we got there. But the deep personal love that He has for us as individuals caused Him to do it Himself! Some Christians have such a high view of God, that they can hardly conceive that God would bother about them as an individual. They reason that the apostle Paul may merit some personal attention from the Most High God, but not them. But Scripture is so plain; Jesus said that He was preparing a place for us. Why not believe it, and enjoy the thrill of it?

Think what it cost Him to open the way into Heaven for us. Calvary shows us the cost if we care to consider that great sacrifice for a while. If He has paid such a price for our salvation, then it is indeed an insult to neglect this great truth of Heaven. Firstly, the barrier of sin had to be removed. God hates sin, and he will have nothing to do with those who persist in it. But He decided to make it possible for the humble to have their sins done away with – the barrier was removed. This is what Jesus did on the Cross – *having cancelled the written code, with its regulations, that was against us and that stood opposed to us; he took it away, nailing it to the cross* (Colossians 2:14). The removal of this barrier opened the way for God to forgive our sins. God cannot live with sin, how then could God allow anything into Heaven which would spoil it? Sin would do so. God made up His mind that Heaven would be a perfect place, so, sinners were out! **But** God *so loved the world* that He decided to draw men to Himself, and to make them fit to enter such a beautiful place. He made it possible for us to be forgiven. *Jesus said, 'Father, **forgive them**, for they do not know what they are doing'* (Luke 23:34). The Father responded by agreeing to do so.

16

Consider the depth of His longing to have us with Him there

Father, I want those you have given me to be with me where I am, and to see my glory, the glory you have given me because you loved me before the creation of the world (John 17:24). You may feel sometimes that God does not care about you, but this verse proves the opposite. He wants you as close as possible to Himself, **forever**! If God has such a strong desire to have you in Heaven, and if He has gone to such lengths to make it possible, how can we neglect ... *such a great salvation?* (Hebrews 2:3). And how can we despise such a great Heavenly Home?

A dear friend of mine, whose evangelistic fervour I greatly admire, and whose preaching has brought many into the Kingdom, said in a sermon 'I don't want to go to Heaven, only Satan wants us to get to Heaven.' I understand what he was getting at; he thinks that there are millions who need to hear the Gospel, so we can't be thinking of Heaven yet, there is too much work to do. Laudable in some ways, but a terrible insult to Jesus, who went to such lengths to save the lost and to prepare a home for them.

Many Christians fear Heaven

They neglect to think of Heaven because they fear it. They fear it because they only think of the **mysterious** aspect of Heaven. To us at the moment Heaven **is** somewhat mysterious. The Bible does not give too many clear details about it. But that is one of the things which make it exciting. Just think of the endless discoveries to be made when we get there. The continual fulfilment of learning wonderful new things.

Some Christians only think of the **everlasting** aspect of it. They are afraid of eternity because there seems to be no end to Heaven, and they say 'what do we do if we don't like it!' I have heard Christians ask the question 'if we don't like it there, is there anywhere else to go?' They don't want to go to Hell, but is there anywhere else? It sounds incredible, but people do ask this question.

In some ways Heaven is everlasting and mysterious, but the major thing is that **God is there**. The God who loved us and gave Himself for us. Our dear Father who loves to bless us with every spiritual blessing – *Praise be to the God and Father of our Lord Jesus Christ, who has blessed us in the Heavenly realms with **every spiritual blessing in Christ*** (Ephesians 1:3).

If God is going to be there forever, why should we be afraid? Sadly, many people are afraid. The best thing is to consider the **quality** of life in Heaven more than its extent. It is a life free from limitation of any sort. A life of endless satisfaction. Think about it, and enjoy it in advance, then pray – 'Thank you Lord for opening Heaven to me. Help me to think about Heaven daily.' By doing so, we will avoid disobeying God's command to consider Heaven constantly.

Chapter 2

Who will be in Heaven?

If we have repented of our sin of neglecting to think about Heaven, we may find ourselves asking the question 'who will be in Heaven?' The best way to find out is to look into Scripture. The Bible declares that it is **only** those who are born again who are in Heaven. Those who are born again are welcome there because in Heaven they are at Home. All the hard labour, trials, frustrations and limitations of earth are gone forever. We are where we have really belonged since we were born again. It is as though we lived on earth as expatriates; not really a part of the land where we lived, but longing to be where we really belonged – *But our citizenship is in Heaven. And we eagerly await a Saviour from there, the Lord Jesus Christ* (Philippians 3:20).

Not everyone agrees with my statement that it is only those who are born again who will be in Heaven, particularly those who believe in the heresy known as Universalism. Those who preach it believe that everyone will be saved in the end. Heaven will be open to all mankind. Those who believe the heresy of Universalism emphasise God's love, not His righteousness. Origen was one, even though he was said to be a great evangelist! Universalists say that death is simply the way to life, and punishment is only a remedy which might possibly be needed for a short time. In which case salvation comes through judgement. Their belief is that the Law came before Gospel, so keeping the Law or living a good life does away with the demands of the Gospel. As for eternity, they say that the word 'eternal' can mean a block of time, which **may** be eternal. Their belief is in the reconciliation of all things, irrespective of the condition of man's heart. They cite the Scripture – *and through him to reconcile to himself all things, whether things on earth or things in heaven, by making peace through his blood, shed on the cross* (Colossians 1:20). They miss the point entirely. It is an attractive theory, until we consider the horrors which Jesus had to endure at Calvary, and the hatred which God has for sin. If men and women prefer to live their life without God, then He will let them do so. If they then expect God to open Heaven to them when they die, they completely misunderstand what Jesus said – *I am the way and the truth and the life. No one comes to the Father except through me* (John 14:6). His dogmatism is not arrogant, but truthful. Who else lived a perfect life amidst all the temptations that we have to endure? Who else endured Calvary because he love mankind so deeply? Where is the man or woman who deserves to by-pass Calvary and enter Heaven because their life was so perfect?

Heaven is an exclusive place

God has decreed that – *Nothing impure will ever enter it, nor will anyone who does what is shameful or deceitful, but only those whose names are written in the Lamb's book of life* (Revelation 21:27). Those who do good works but reject the Lordship of Christ will never get in to Heaven. The good works argument is one of the most common attempts to reject what I have just written. Most of us have heard people say 'I live a good life; I care for my neighbours; I pay my taxes.' All this may be true, but it does not impress God. He refutes it in Scripture – *All of us have become like one who is unclean, and all our righteous acts are like filthy rags; we all shrivel up like a leaf, and like the wind our sins sweep us away* (Isaiah 64:6). If we want to get to Heaven by good works, hear what Jesus said to the Pharisees who were expert in good works – *For I tell you that unless your right-eousness surpasses that of the Pharisees and the teachers of the law, you will certainly not enter the kingdom of heaven* (Matthew 5:20). If we want to get to Heaven by obeying God's Laws, hear what James said – *For whoever keeps the whole law and yet stumbles at just one point is guilty of breaking all of it* (James 2:10). The thing which makes the good works argument so offensive to God is the fact that it is really an attempt to bypass Calvary, and to avoid God's demand for total surrender. Our will is the very last thing we yield to God! My question is – can anyone refuse to surrender to God in the light of Calvary?

But there are some questions that people ask about those who will be in Heaven. One question is –

Will suicides be in Heaven?

If the one who committed suicide was not a Christian, the question does not apply. But if the person was a Christian, then, because suicide is self murder, this must bring some kind of loss at the Judgement Seat. *For we must all appear before the judgment seat of Christ, that each one may receive what is due him for the **things done while in the body**, whether good **or bad*** (2 Corinthians 5:10). But it is likely that the one who committed suicide will suffer a loss of rewards, but not a loss of salvation. Suicide cuts short our destiny down here, but it does not invalidate regeneration. *I give them **eternal** life, and they shall never perish; no one can snatch them out of my hand* (John 10:28).

Another common question is –

Will babies be in Heaven?

Some scholars say that – 'All who die in infancy are saved.' This is inferred from the Scripture, *Consequently, just as the result of one trespass was condemnation for all men, so also the result of one act of righteousness was justification that brings life for **all men*** (Romans 5:18). They say that this includes babies. Furthermore, these scholars say 'The Scriptures nowhere exclude any class of infants, baptized or unbaptized, born in Christian or heathen lands, of believing or unbelieving parents from the benefits of redemption in Christ' (Charles Hodge. *Systematic Theology*. Vol. 1. p. 26).

My personal view is that life begins at conception, although others believe that life begins when a baby takes its first breath. When I speak of babies going to Heaven when they die, I define a baby as one who has not reached the age of responsibility. This is difficult to define because intelligence varies in individual babies, so I will not attempt to define it here! There are parents who believe that their children go to Heaven because they (the parents) are Christians. I do not believe that is necessarily true, but the children of Christian parents may have a better chance of finding salvation than others. However, this is another problem area and this book is not specifically addressing such issues in detail.

I feel it is important to stress that neither babies nor children are innocent. We must beware of sentimentality in which we say that dear little children are so innocent. They are not. Some years ago at an open air service, an atheist was jeering at a Professor of Theology. He said 'surely you don't believe in original sin? How can you prove such a thing?' The professor replied, 'It is simple; I have four children.' Any parent will understand what he meant! My own belief is that children are not saved because they are innocent. Scripture says that they are not innocent. *Surely I was* **sinful at birth**, *sinful from the time my mother conceived me* (Psalm 51:5). *For **all** have sinned and fall short of the glory of God* (Romans 3:23). *All of us also lived among them at one time, gratifying the cravings of our sinful nature and following its desires and thoughts. Like the rest, we were **by nature** objects of wrath* (Ephesians 2:3).

I personally believe that if a baby dies it goes to be with God. But children are saved by the **grace of God alone**. My reasoning takes in the attitude of Jesus towards children. In it, there is the desire to save them, and His grace goes out towards them. *Jesus said, 'Let the little children come to me, and do not hinder them, for the kingdom of heaven belongs to such as these'* (Matthew 19:14). He had a great regard for children, and uttered an awful prophecy against those who would harm them. *But if anyone causes one of these little ones who believe in me to sin, it would be better for him to have a large* **millstone** *hung around his neck and to be drowned in the depths of the sea* (Matthew 18:6). If God cares so deeply for children, including babies, it is very unlikely that He would cast then into Hell when they die. I do not believe that children remain children when they are in Heaven. Children are immature, and undeveloped, and there cannot be any immaturity or retarded development in Heaven. A friend of mine says that we will all be about thirty three years of age, because Jesus was, and we have a body *like His glorious body*. It may be true! My point is really that babies do go to Heaven, by the grace of God, but they are raised from death with a body or being capable of ruling with God. And yet we will still recognise them, as I have said in 'What is Heaven Like?'

Some ask the question 'Do the mentally handicapped go to Heaven?' My belief is the mentally handicapped need the same Gospel as anyone else, but if they respond in faith as far as they can within their limitations, then God will respond to them, and save them. Not all those who are handicapped will respond, but many do. God can reach the depths of a person's being, whatever their capacity. He can regenerate a small child; one of our children was soundly born again at the age of three. In any case He foresees what decision a person would make.

The danger of presumption

I do not want to shake anyone's faith, but on the other hand I am concerned about the shallow 'believism' which is prevalent today. So I venture to say that there are many people in our churches who, although they know the songs, recite Scriptures, come to the prayer meetings, are in fact not really born again. There is room for caution in our assessment of those who purport to be Christians. If someone professes to be a Christian we should look for the signs. If they are really convicted of sin and their need of God; if they cry out for mercy; if they surrender totally to God; and if they show the hallmarks of regeneration, and rapidly get rid of old habits, then we can be sure that the Scripture has become true, *Therefore, if anyone is in Christ, he is a new creation; the old has gone, the new has come!* (2 Corinthians 5:17). Such people will rarely if ever abandon themselves to a life of sin. Their love for God will ensure that although they may slip back from time to time, they will not desert the Lord whom they love. I believe that if we are truly born again, we are likely to continue to the end. God says some wonderful things about such people: *Blessed is the man who does not fall away on account of me* (Matthew 11:6); *but he who stands firm to the end will be saved* (Matthew 24:13); *To those who by **persistence** in doing good seek glory, honour and immortality, he will give eternal life* (Romans 2:7).

There does seem to be a possibility of apostasy (falling away) for false professions (not truly born again), so let us beware of easy believism. Scripture seems quite plain about the possibility of falling away. *At that time many will turn away from the faith and will betray and hate each other, and many false prophets will appear and deceive many people. Because of the increase of wickedness, the love of most will grow cold* (Matthew 24:10–12). We have our wretched old nature to contend with, often hindering us in our walk with God. In addition we have an enemy who hates us and will do anything to turn us away from our love for God. But, we also have the power of the Holy Spirit to help us. If we had to depended solely on our own strength and determination to keep going, we should be without hope, I personally believe that if we are truly born again, we will persevere to the end, but it will be completely because of His help. Be encouraged by the Scriptures – *being confident of this, that he who began a good work in you will carry it on to completion until the day of Christ Jesus* (Philippians 1:6). *He will keep you strong to the end, so that you will be blameless on the day of our Lord Jesus Christ* (1 Corinthians 1:8). God gives us everything we need in order to persevere to the end. *His divine power has given us everything we need for life and godliness through our knowledge of him who called us by his own glory and goodness* (2 Peter 1:3). Thank God for that! But the fact that God offers us all we need highlights the fact that there is no excuse for refusing it! How wonderful it is to have such a hope within us ...

Chapter 3

The Christian's Hope

The word 'hope' has changed its meaning today

If we have made sure that we have received eternal life from
Jesus, and if we have surrendered our life to Him as Lord,
then we can know that we will be among those in Heaven to
which I have just referred. We can begin to rejoice in our
great hope. What a lovely word it is. Originally as in the
Bible, the word hope meant that which is sure and certain;
it meant confident expectation. It was something on which
we could depend. But in today's usage hope means something that **might** come about; something about which we
are slightly **un**certain. We say 'perhaps it will come about,
but we are not sure.' But, Christians believe the Bible meaning of the word 'hope'. Our hope has certainty in it. It is a
word which inspires confidence in us.

Our hope of Heaven is a *living* hope

Consider the Scripture – *Praise be to the God and Father of
our Lord Jesus Christ! In his great mercy he has given us new
birth into **a living hope** through the resurrection of Jesus
Christ from the dead* (1 Peter 1:3). This hope is the hope of
Heaven – being with God forever. It is only Christians who
have real hope. This is one of the things that distinguish
them from the unsaved. Without God there is no hope.

26

With God there is hope. Before I was born again, I was hopeless, helpless and afraid. The Bible describes me as I was – *remember that at that time you were separate from Christ, excluded from citizenship in Israel and foreigners to the covenants of the promise, without hope and without God in the world* (Ephesians 2:12). But now that I am a child of God, I have a hope and I am **not** like those who are hopeless – *Brothers, we do not want you to be ignorant about those who fall asleep, or to grieve like the rest of men, **who have no hope*** (1 Thessalonians 4:13). Christians have hope, but this is not because they are better than non-Christians for *all have sinned and fall short of the glory of God* (Romans 3:23). But because they have fled to God and obtained the hope of salvation. Pity those without this hope. What are we doing about them?

Christians are tomorrow's people. We have a hope and a future. No wonder we look forward to Jesus coming again. Our testimony is: *we wait for the blessed hope – the glorious appearing of our great God and Saviour, Jesus Christ* (Titus 2:13). Those who are being persecuted in some parts of the world have their faith sorely tested, but this hope sustains them. God has promised that He will come again and take them to glory. There is no reason why we in the UK should not be tested by persecution. What is so special about our nation that it should not be subject to such trouble? God utilises it to make us more pure than we are, and persecution certainly sorts out the true Christian from the false, and it strengthens the faith of those who remain true to God when it is hard to do so. It also helps God's people to fix their attention on Heaven more than they did before. Persecuted or not, it is good to anticipate our great hope of Heaven. One of my friends sent me this letter from Dr Harry Rimmer to his friend Dr Charles Fuller. It focuses on our great hope of Heaven:

'I believe you are going to speak about Heaven next Sunday. I am interested in that land because I have held a clear title to a bit of property there for about fifty years. I didn't buy it, it was given to me without price, but the Donor purchased it for me at a tremendous sacrifice. I'm not holding it for speculation, it's not a vacant lot. For more than half a century I've been sending materials up to the greatest Architect in the universe, Who has been building a home for me, which will never need re-modelling, because it will suit me perfectly and will never grow old. Termites can never undermine its foundations, for it rests on the Rock of Ages; fire cannot destroy it, floods cannot wash it away; no bolts will ever be placed upon the doors, for no vicious person will ever enter the land where my dwelling stands. It's almost completed and almost ready for me to enter in and abide in peace eternally without fear of being ejected. There is a valley of deep shadow between this place where I live and that to which I shall journey in a short time. I cannot reach my home in that City without passing through this valley. But I'm not afraid because the best friend I ever had went through that same valley long long ago, and drove away all its gloom. He has stuck with me through thick and thin since we first became acquainted 55 years ago. And I own His promise in printed form, never to forsake me or leave me alone. He will be with me as I walk through the valley of the shadow. And I shall not lose my way when He is with me. My ticket to Heaven has no date marked for the journey; no return coupon; no permit for baggage. I'm ready to go and I may not be here when you are talking next Sunday evening but I will meet you there some day.'

Harry Rimmer died before the Sunday.

Hope is in our hearts now. It will be fulfilled later ...

We already have the hope in our hearts while we are here on earth – *through whom we have gained access by faith into this*

28

*grace in which we **now stand**. And we rejoice in the **hope** of the glory of God* (Romans 5:2). But our hope is not only for this life, we could be very miserable if that were true; as the Bible says – *If only for this life we have **hope** in Christ, we are to be pitied more than all men* (1 Corinthians 15:19).

Our hope is indeed a hope that keeps us strong and confident in this life, but our hope will turn to certainty when we get to Heaven – *the faith and love that spring from the **hope** that is **stored up for you in heaven** and that you have already heard about in the word of truth, the gospel* (Colossians 1:5). God wants us to **know** (be intimately acquainted with) this great hope. God the Holy Spirit has come to answer Paul's prayer for Christians everywhere. He prayed – *that the eyes of your heart may be enlightened in order that you may **know** the **hope** to which he has called you, the riches of his glorious inheritance in the saints* (Ephesians 1:18). The more we consider this great hope of ours, the stronger it will become in our hearts. Then we shall press on with our work for God more enthusiastically than ever. God put hope into our hearts when we were born again, and as part of that experience of being born again He imparted His own nature to us. This includes hope because he is a God of hope. The Bible says so – *May the **God of hope** fill you with all joy and peace as you trust in him, so that you may overflow with **hope** by the power of the Holy Spirit* (Romans 15:13). But it is up to us to **maintain** our hope. God will not do what we can do; He will not do our homework for us, we must constantly meditate on our great hope of Heaven as seen in the Bible; Scripture is full of it. However, if the Spirit of God sees us diligently meditating on our hope of Heaven, He will come and add His inspiration to our meditation, and the result will be an uplifting in our hearts, and a **living** hope in them.

We can lose our sense of expectancy of getting to Heaven if we are not careful. So God, in His Word warns us to persist – *if you **continue in your faith**, established and firm, not moved from the **hope** held out in the gospel* (Colossians 1:23). It demands patience, because Jesus is not here yet, though He will not be long. Meanwhile, let us think about our hope – talk about it – and thank God for it – *while we wait for the blessed hope – the glorious appearing of our great God and Saviour, Jesus Christ* (Titus 2:13). It takes discipline, but it is worth it!

What is this hope?

Seeing that I write elsewhere in detail about all these aspects of our hope, I only mention them briefly here, together with a relevant Scripture.

Hope of resurrection

... and I have the same hope in God as these men, that there will be a resurrection of both the righteous and the wicked (Acts 24:15).

Hope of salvation

But since we belong to the day, let us be self-controlled, putting on faith and love as a breastplate, and the hope of salvation as a helmet (1 Thessalonians 5:8). Salvation includes everything that God is going to give us. This includes an eternal Home, a new body, re-union with those we love, and service in the Kingdom, to name only some of these blessings.

Hope of His Coming

Scripture puts words to our longings – *Come, O Lord!* (1 Corinthians 16:22). And Jesus replies to us – *He who testifies to these things says, 'Yes, I am coming soon.'* And we repeat our prayer *Amen. Come, Lord Jesus* (Revelation 22:20).

Our hope affects our conduct

Our hope strengthens us

Contemplating our hope of Heaven is a practical thing to do. It is not idling away our time at all. It has several effects. One is to keep us calm and assured in a world in turmoil. *We have this **hope** as **an anchor for the soul**, firm and secure* (Hebrews 6:19). The 'hope' in this verse is our hope of salvation. In an uncertain age, and a bewildering world where nothing seems to be stable or assured, it is a great source of strength to have such a hope. It keeps us going in our work for God. The old hymn by Edward Mote puts it well – 'My hope is built on nothing less, than Jesus' blood and righteousness ... on Christ the solid Rock I stand ... dressed in His righteousness alone, faultless to stand before His Throne' (Redemption Hymnal).

Our hope can help to maintain our purity

*Everyone who has this **hope** in him **purifies himself**, just as he is pure* (1 John 3:3). Everyone who expects an important visitor will get themselves ready for them. To be clean and tidy is a form of courtesy and respect. When the 'visitor' is Jesus, we will certainly want to be spiritually 'clean and tidy' for Him. Who wants to be blushing when God comes for His people!

Our hope causes us to rejoice

Be joyful in hope, patient in affliction, faithful in prayer (Romans 12:12). The news programmes do not bring us much joy. Indeed there seems to be a settled policy in many of our news networks of bringing those things that are evil, hurtful, or depressing. Christians have a defence against that, because our hope is that of a new world where evil is unknown.

The hope must be communicated

How can Christians refrain from speaking about the greatest hope in the world? We may be shy, but that is no excuse for keeping silent about Heaven. People want to know. Even those so-called macho men who sneer about heaven when they are in a crowd, on a one-to-one basis often confess to a fear of the eternal future. Let us tell them; after all the Bible is very explicit – *But in your hearts set apart Christ as Lord. Always **be prepared to give an answer** to everyone who asks you to give the reason for the hope that you have. But do this with gentleness and respect* (1 Peter 3:15). Since we have such a hope – the only hope for this world, we dare not be selfish with it. Surely we love God dearly enough to communicate to others whom He would love to bring into Heaven!

Having spoken at some length about this great hope of Heaven, let us find out where it is. Turn to the next chapter please.

Chapter 4

Where is Heaven?

We have the hope of Heaven in our hearts, so we are bound to wonder where this wonderful place is. Heaven may be a place, a sphere, or a dimension. Paul did not know how to describe it accurately. As he said – *I know a man in Christ who fourteen years ago was caught up to the **third heaven**. Whether it was in the body or out of the body I do not know – God knows. And I know that this man – whether in the body or apart from the body I do not know, but God knows – was caught up to **paradise**. He heard inexpressible things, things that man is not permitted to tell* (2 Corinthians 12:2–4).

Heaven may be nearer to us than we think. In fact Scripture says this – **he is not far from each one of us** (Acts 17:27). We need to remember this during times of loneliness, or bereavement, or severe trial. He is not 'up there' – miles away from our situation. He is near you, with you, and for you. I used to think of Heaven as a huge box somewhere up in the sky, which, according to my elders was made of gold, and was 1500 miles square. I thought that when we died we all went into this box forever. No wonder I was scared of Heaven! I am not scared of Heaven now, but I still have one problem – it is this – if Heaven is God's home, and yet He is everywhere, then where is Heaven? For example, God is in us if we are born again, but we cannot say therefore that we are Heaven! However, I do not want to speculate too much, and I confess my limited understanding. So now let us look at the different terms used in the Bible about Heaven.

Heaven

Heaven is where God is

When Jesus taught His disciples to pray, He said that we should address our prayers to His Father who is in Heaven. *This, then, is how you should pray: 'Our Father in heaven, hallowed be your name'* (Matthew 6:9). Jesus repeated it when He said to us *In the same way, let your light shine before men, that they may see your good deeds and praise your Father in Heaven* (Matthew 5:16). I add two Scriptures here to illustrate Heaven as both a location and a vast realm. Firstly, *'Do not I fill Heaven and earth?' declares the* LORD (Jeremiah 23:24). Secondly, *This is what the* LORD *says: 'Heaven is my throne, and the earth is my footstool...'* (Isaiah 66:1). One minute God says that His Throne is in Heaven, and the next minute he says that Heaven is His Throne! Perhaps the answer is that God is so great that His Throne, or Home is bound to be large enough to dominate Creation. He is a real Person, therefore He must be somewhere, it seems to me that He has decided to be in Heaven, but He is not limited to any location. For the moment I will regard Heaven as a location – God's home – and the Heavenly places as the environs of it – the vast realm or domain (see 'Domain' in chapter 14, 'The Kingdom').

Heaven is where God's Throne is

When Isaiah, Ezekiel, and John looked into Heaven, they saw the likeness of God on a Throne. It was only His likeness that they saw – a faint glimpse of His radiance. If they had seen God in all His glory they would have died on the spot. God made this plain when Moses asked God to show him His glory. *'But,'* he said, *'you cannot see my face, for no one may see me and live'* (Exodus 33:20). (By the way, when we are in Heaven, we **will** see His glory, and we will **not** die because we will have new minds with which we will be able to bear the sight of His glory.)

Have you ever seen this Throne in a vision? It is a very large Throne; angels crowd around it, standing like coiled springs, ready to go on any errand for God. They wait for His command, and at the first syllable from His lips they are off to do His will. Through all Creation they serve Him, including on the earth. I wonder how often they have come to safeguard us – to stand between us and a another vehicle on our motorways. How often have they stood around our homes when evil was intended? From this Throne angels came and fed Elijah in his dark cave. One of the interesting things in Heaven will be the record of how God has kept us and provided for us through the ministry of angels. More about them in chapter 13 – 'Activities of Angels'.

God rules from this Throne. When a command went out from this Throne to bring down the Roman empire, it fell. Another command from the Throne ensured the end of the Greek, Persian, and other empires when they had served God's purposes. The British Empire was raised up by God, but when it dishonoured God, He brought it down. It was from this Throne that the command went out to redeem mankind, and on that occasion it was Jesus who left it in order to die and rise again. 'Thank you Lord Jesus that you came, and thank you Father that you allowed Him to come. Thank you Holy Spirit for empowering Jesus to save us.'

Heaven is the Family home for Christians

Christians are the children of God, loved and wanted by Him. Loved by Him wholeheartedly, unconditionally, and continually.

John said we are God's children – *to all who received him, to those who believed in his name, he gave the right to become children of God* (John 1:12).

God the Holy Spirit said so – *The Spirit himself testifies with our spirit that we are God's children* (Romans 8:16).

35

God the Father said so – *'I will be a Father to you, and you will be my sons and daughters, says the Lord Almighty'* (2 Corinthians 6:18).

Seeing that we are God's children, we have a Family Home – in Heaven where God lives.

Heaven is where Satan used to be

Satan used to be in heaven, but when pride came into his heart and he tried to de-throne God, he was thrown out by God – *And there was war in Heaven. Michael and his angels fought against the dragon, and the dragon and his angels fought back. But he was not strong enough, and they lost their place in heaven. The great dragon was hurled down – that ancient serpent called the devil, or Satan, who leads the whole world astray. He was hurled to the earth, and his angels with him* (Revelation 12:7–9). He will never be allowed back!

Environs – The Heavens

There are cloudy Heavens

Look at the birds of the air (Matthew 6:26). Birds fly in the visible Heavens or sky.

These are the Heavens which we can see with our eyes, and which we fly through on our air travels.

There are starry Heavens

... the sun and the moon and all the stars of the heavens... (Jeremiah 8:2); *The stars of heaven and their constellations ... The rising sun ... the moon.* (Isaiah 13:10); *the stars ... and the Heavenly bodies...* (Mark 13:25).

These are the Heavens which we see through our telescopes.

Environs – Heavenly places

The Heavens and the Heavenly places may be one and the same. I do not know for sure, and it does not matter too much. The main thing is that it is all under the control of God, even though it **seems** to be under the devil's control sometimes. So, let us explain as far as we can. Heavenly places are –

Where spiritual rulers sit

There are evil powers in the Heavenly places. The good powers are in Heaven attending God, but they travel anywhere to serve Him. For example, they come into the Heavenly places to fight against the evil powers as in Daniel's time (see Daniel chapter 10). These good angels rejoice as we give a good demonstration of godliness upon the earth. The Bible speaks about this – *His intent was that now, through the church, the manifold wisdom of God* should be made known to the *rulers and authorities in the Heavenly realms* (Ephesians 3:10). Of course, the evil powers in heavenly places are angered and frustrated as we do so, for they are our enemies – *For our struggle is not against flesh and blood, but against the rulers, against the authorities, against the powers of this dark world and against the spiritual forces of evil in the Heavenly realms* (Ephesians 6:12).

God created them all

Whether we talk about Heaven, Heavens, or Heavenly places, Jesus created them all. The Bible plainly says, *In the beginning, O Lord, you laid the foundations of the earth, and the Heavens are the work of your hands* (Hebrews 1:10). I believe that this term 'Heavens' includes them all. God created them all – He is in touch with them all – He controls them all. *He who descended is the very one who ascended higher than all the Heavens, in order to fill the whole universe* (Ephesians 4:10).

I want now to disregard the terms 'Heavens', and 'the Heavenlies' or 'Heavenly places' for a while, and concentrate on Heaven itself.

Heaven is where Jesus sits at the moment

He is back there now; where He came from; where He belongs, and has always belonged, on the Throne! He is back having accomplished the sacrifice for sin – the demolition of Satan's power, and the plan of salvation. (God) *raised him from the dead and seated him at his right hand in the Heavenly realms ... far above all rule and authority, power and dominion, and every title that can be given, not only in the present age but also in the one to come* (Ephesians 1:20–21). Notice that Jesus is seated.

This is a sign that His great work is finished, successful, complete. Triumphant. Kings always sat down when they had conquered. Notice too that Jesus is at God's right hand. This is the place of highest honour, the seat for the favourite. (Jesus) *who has gone into Heaven and is at God's right hand – with angels, authorities and powers in submission to him* (1 Peter 3:22). At the moment Jesus is still in Heaven. The angel told them that He was there – '... *Jesus, who has been taken from you into Heaven, will come back in the same way you have seen him go into Heaven'* (Acts 1:11). But He will be back!

It is where Jesus prays for us now

It is a great encouragement for us to know that Jesus is praying for us at this moment – *but because Jesus lives forever, he has a permanent priesthood. Therefore he is able to save completely those who come to God through him, because he always lives to intercede for them* (Hebrews 7:24, 25). *Who is he that condemns? Christ Jesus, who died – more than that, who was raised to life – is at the right hand of God and is also interceding for us* (Romans 8:34). As God looks over the earth, He sees our situations, and knows our needs. He is willing to supply our needs and to intervene in our situations. But He has decided to work together with His dear Son. So, He listens to the prayers of Jesus as well as our prayers; when He hears ours and finds them in line with those of Jesus, He answers them. With such an

Intercessor, how can we lose! It will be wonderful when we get to Heaven to hear the prayers that Jesus has prayed for us while on earth. Who knows how greatly they have benefited us in our work and warfare! At the moment we don't know, but in Heaven we will know.

It is where we 'sit' at this moment

The Bible says that *God raised us up with Christ and seated us with him in the Heavenly realms in Christ Jesus* (Ephesians 2:6). What does it mean to *sit with Him*...? Obviously we are on the earth at this moment and God is in Heaven, but our spirits are alive to God, and we are in contact with Him. In our spirit we speak to Him, we listen to Him, and we are near to Him. This is how we are *sitting with Him*. Many Christians have difficulty with the thought that we are 'sitting' on the same throne on which God sits. They ask how it is possible; they regard it as virtual blasphemy to say such things. But what else can this verse mean? Jesus sits on that throne and the Bible plainly says that He has raised us up to sit with Him. Where else can we be 'sitting'? I still tremble a bit at the immensity of this thought, but I have decided to believe it, enjoy it, and make sure that I am clean enough to do so. God, Who is surrounded by angels, Seraphim, and Cherubim, looks at us, wants us to come nearer and in a prophecy given to me says to His angels –

'make way for My servants, all My servants are kings and queens – move aside and let them come nearer to Me. Come near My dear ones and if any of you need to be cleansed, then kneel before Me, but do not grovel. Confess your sin, be cleansed afresh and then come and sit on the Throne where you belong. This is your Home where you will be forever. But learn to sit here now so that I can share with you the secrets of eternity. Look across from here, and overhear the plans of the evil powers as they direct the demons upon the earth. Then hear My strategy, and through it, let us destroy their strategy upon the earth.'

How big is Heaven?

I cannot believe that Heaven is smaller than Creation, and Creation is vast. Think how vast it is! Our earthly systems of measurement are inadequate to express Creation distances. A spaceship travelling at 100,000 miles per hour would take 670 million years to cross the Milky Way. There are 100,000 million stars in it. In addition, the astronomers tell us that there are 2000 million Galaxies like ours. The star nearest to earth is Proxima Centauri. If a man could travel at 35,000 miles per hour, it would take him over 80 years to get to it. To explore such wonders we need both a new body capable of coping with different conditions, and the 'time' to do it. This is only possible to those who are heading for Heaven. If Heaven is a dimension, then these illustrations give some idea of its scale! I used to wonder if there would be room for all Christians to squeeze into Heaven – I don't now!

Will Heaven last forever?

The Heaven we speak about now is not actually the final Heaven or perhaps we should say that it is not Heaven in its final renewed form. Jesus said, *Heaven and earth will pass away, but my words will never pass away* (Matthew 24:35). John said, *Then I saw a **new** heaven and a new earth, for the first heaven and the first earth had passed away, and there was no longer any sea* (Revelation 21:1).

Wonderful though Heaven is now, it seems that in some way God will make it even better, or should we say 'different'. There is certainly going to be some change in the Heavens. *By the same word the **present** Heavens and earth are reserved for fire, being kept for the day of judgement and destruction of ungodly men* (2 Peter 3:7). *But the day of the Lord will come like a thief. The **Heavens** will disappear with a roar; the elements will be destroyed by fire, and the earth and everything in it will be laid bare . . .* (2 Peter 3:10). Perhaps we should not worry too much about the details of these changes, but make sure that we will be with God – then we will find out the whole truth about the matter.

There will be a new Heaven

*But in keeping with his promise we are looking forward to a **new Heaven** and a new earth, the home of righteousness* (2 Peter 3:13). *Then I saw **a new Heaven** and a new earth, for the first Heaven and the first earth had passed away, and there was no longer any sea* (Revelation 21:1). W. Hendriksen says,

> 'It is the same Heaven and earth, but gloriously rejuvenated ... the old order has vanished ... all Creation's potential is now fully realised.'
>
> (*More than Conquerors*. p. 198. Tynedale Press)

So there will be a new Heaven and earth, which I believe will be one inseparable realm really. This will be ... *put into effect when the times will have reached their fulfilment – to bring all things in **Heaven** and on earth together under one head, even Christ* (Ephesians 1:10). This Heaven is described as the New Jerusalem. The place where the church and God are together. *But you have come to Mount Zion, to the Heavenly Jerusalem, the city of the living God. You have come to thousands upon thousands of angels in joyful assembly* (Hebrews 12:22). Whether we speak about the present Heaven or the New Heaven, we are sure of two things. Firstly, we will be with God. Secondly, God is eternal, therefore He will always be with us, and we will always be with Him. So, we need not get too involved in the details of the Old and the New Heaven. However, we want to find out as much as we can so that when we arrive, it will not be too much of a shock. Bearing in mind that we must not let our imagination run away with us, let us see what we can find out about Heaven from the Bible. I try to describe it in two instalments: one in the next chapter – 'What is Heaven Like?' and the second in chapter 14 – 'The Kingdom'.

Chapter 5

What is Heaven Like?

God has not given us clear details as to what it is like in Heaven, therefore none of us know everything about it. I certainly do not. But we can share what we do know, and we can make suggestions about those things which seem unclear. For the sake of clarity in this chapter I will use the term Heaven. Chapter 14 on 'The Kingdom of Heaven' describes other aspects of the term (in it I use the phrase 'Heaven is a location, God's Home, and a vast realm or domain'). The events I mention may take place in either the Location or the Realm, but the main thing is that they will be real and actual events. Some things seem to overlap, and it is not easy to write about things in which Scripture does not go into detail. But, as I said at the start, I want to enthuse us more with the prospect of Heaven than trying to work out the details.

God is in Heaven

Having written in the previous chapter about those who will be in Heaven, I want to re-state what I wrote in chapter 4 – 'Where is Heaven', the obvious, but most important fact – God will be there. In fact Heaven is Heaven because God is there. In Heaven we are in the Presence of God. Without Him, there could not be a Heaven. Even on earth it is people who make places. The atmosphere in Heaven is determined by the character of God. Because God is peace, joy, love, purity etc., that is the atmosphere of His Home. We will not spoil it, because He has already imparted His character to us here and now. We will manifest it in even greater measure there.

Jesus looks forward to our presence in Heaven. In fact He has been preparing it for us. *In my Father's house are many rooms; if it were not so, I would have told you. I am going there to prepare a place for you* (John 14:2). When you feel unimportant, and Satan tries to make you feel even worse, just remember that Jesus, God the Son, is personally getting ready for you to join Him! He must love us, and want us if He has gone to such trouble to receive us there. This is evident in His great prayer – *'Father, I want those you have given me to be with me where I am, and to see my glory, the glory you have given me because you loved me before the creation of the world'* (John 17:24). Surely the deep longing in His heart is mirrored in ours? If not, it shows the shallowness of our love for Him. All true lovers long to be together.

We will see God, and we will be like God

After our death, our spirits will be conscious and 'with Christ', for the spirit does not need the body in order to function. Many of the things which I mention below will only happen in their fullness when we have our new bodies. But when we receive them after the Resurrection, all that I describe will be literally fulfilled. Directly we die, we see God. *And I – in righteousness **I shall see your face**; when I awake, I will be satisfied with seeing your likeness* (Psalm 17:15). The Psalmist had this great desire to see God consciously – *One thing I ask of the LORD, ... to **gaze upon** the beauty of the LORD and to seek him in his temple* (Psalm 27:4). On earth we can only imagine what He is like; in visions given by the Spirit, we see something of His likeness, but it is rather unsatisfying to those who are in love with God. We want to see more – to see in greater detail, but we can't. However, when we go to Heaven, we shall see Him in all His glory! By then, we will have our new eyes which will be able to see Him without dying on the spot. Without such eyes, we could not bear the sight of His glory – it would be too much for us. Not only will we see God, we shall be **like** God! *Dear friends, now we are children of God, and what we will be has not yet been made known. But we know that when he appears, **we shall be like him**, for we shall see him as he is* (1 John 3:2). I have written more about our Christlikeness in chapter 10 – 'The Wedding of Christ'.

Our questions will be answered

There are many things which do not make sense in our experience down here. We ask 'Why did this tragedy happen despite my prayers? 'Why did God keep me waiting for so long before He gave me what He promised? How is it that cruel tyrants were able to murder at will? Why didn't God prevent the earthquake in which His own missionaries were killed?' So many questions; so few answers. But in Heaven we will see the other side of the tapestry. A dear friend of ours who had to resign from ministry because of ill health sent me the following verse. It helped him to persevere despite the trauma of his handicap. It says –

> Not till the loom is silent
> And the shuttles cease to fly
> Will God unroll the canvas
> And explain the reason why
> The dark threads are as needful
> In the Weavers skilful hands
> As the threads of gold and silver
> In the pattern HE has planned.

(Anon.)

The fact is that God will show us how wise He was when it did not look as if He cared at all.

What about memory in Heaven?

In Heaven we will need to remember God's goodness to us while we were on earth in order to praise Him for it. We will all have accurate memories in Heaven, memories that will recall every good thing God did for us. Our spirits will be so alive to God that we will all sing to Him spontaneously, probably composing songs on the spot about His goodness and mercy to us while we were on earth. We will not remember bad things for they are imperfect, and there will be nothing imperfect in Heaven.

So will we remember our former sins? Not if they have been confessed and repented of. They are erased from God's record. He will not remember them again, and with our new mind and body, we will not do so either. *I, even I, am he who **blots out your transgressions**, for my own sake, and remembers your sins no more* (Isaiah 43:25). *Repent, then, and turn to God, so that your sins may be **wiped out**, that times of refreshing may come from the Lord* (Acts 3:19). *If we confess our sins, he is faithful and just and will forgive us our sins and **purify us** from all unrighteousness* (1 John 1:9). What a relief! I don't fancy hearing all my sins read out in the hearing of all in Heaven! But if they are erased, how can they be read out! Remember that there are conditions to forgiveness. Firstly, if we refuse to forgive those who have sinned against us, God will not forgive us. *But if you do not forgive men their sins, your Father will not forgive your sins* (Matthew 6:15). Secondly, we are forgiven if we walk in the light. *But **if we walk in the light**, as he is in the light, we have fellowship with one another, and the blood of Jesus, his Son, purifies us from all sin* (1 John 1:7).

We will surely remember the Bible in Heaven

I believe that we will still have the Bible in Heaven, and the constant discovery and learning in Heaven or the Kingdom of Heaven will include a greater understanding of the Scriptures. I believe that the Bible is so precious that it will be in

Heaven. I believe that the Psalmist refers to the Bible when he says – *Your word, O LORD, is eternal; it stands firm in the Heavens* (Psalm 119:89). Jesus says a similar thing – *Heaven and earth will pass away, but my words will never pass away* (Mark 13:31). One more proof is – *All your words are true; all your righteous laws are eternal* (Psalm 119:160). This is a great relief to me because although I have studied the Bible for nearly fifty years, I am still frustrated as I try to understand some parts of it. Do you understand Daniel's 70th week, or the whole of the Book of Revelation? Have you worked out what is meant by the verse – *God made him who had no sin to be sin for us, so that in him we might become the righteousness of God* (2 Corinthians 5:21)? There are so many things to understand in Scripture, and although I value my friends who are scholars, and have learned much from them, I still need to hear from those who actually wrote the Scriptures. How wonderful then to get into Moses' seminars on the Pentateuch, or Daniel's on the visions of God. Obadiah's should be good! (Have you read his Book?) Today's plethora of Bible versions are a mixed blessing. I am using the NIV in this book. I don't like it altogether, but it seems to be the most commonly used at the moment. One problem arising from this plethora is – from which version shall we memorise Scripture? At the moment we all have access to the Bible, but when persecution comes to the UK we may be imprisoned and be deprived of our Bibles. If we have not memorised the Word, we are going to be pretty desperate with nothing to keep our mind and heart focused on God. We must read more Scripture in our meetings. We must urge our people to memorise Scripture more than we do. Reciting the Catechism does no harm either!

We will have a new body in Heaven

None of the wonderful activities in Heaven which I have described would be possible if we only had our old bodies. But we won't have them for they were not perfect. Jesus promised a new body to us. He told Paul to write it down for us, and Paul did. He wrote – *it is sown a natural body, it is raised a **spiritual body**. If there is a natural body, there is also a spiritual body* (1 Corinthians 15:44). *And just as we have borne the likeness of the earthly man, so shall we bear the likeness of the man from Heaven* (1 Corinthians 15:49). While He was on earth Jesus was a real man, with all the limitations that we are subject to. He could not walk through doors, nor ascend to Heaven in a flash, nor do without sleep or food constantly. But when He rose from the dead, He had a different body – an immortal body, subject to no limitations. He could ascend to Heaven in a flash; he could walk through doors. When he met the disciples He said to them – *Look at my hands and my feet. It is I myself! Touch me and see; a ghost does not have **flesh and bones**, as you see I have* (Luke 24:39). He did not say 'flesh and **blood**'. To use the word 'blood' would indicate a natural body, a corruptible body. His resurrection body was a different body, incapable of corruption or deterioration in any way. This is the sort of body that He will give us at the Resurrection! God knew very well that we would not be able to function in Heaven without such a body. How could we live forever with a body that was subject to decay and deterioration?

This new body is not dissimilar to our present bodies in some ways. Jesus was recognisably similar to us in His body before and after His Resurrection. He was not a ghostly or unrecognisable person. *They were startled and frightened, thinking they saw a ghost* (Luke 24:37). *When he had said this, he showed them his hands and feet* (Luke 24:40). I believe that our new bodies in Heaven will be like His – *who, by the power that enables him to bring everything under his control, will transform our lowly bodies so that they will be like his glorious body* (Philippians 3:21).

They will be similar to our earthly bodies, though, of course, free from all limitation and imperfection. I cannot believe that God spent all that time designing these bodies, only to discard their basic design and start all over again. Therefore, I expect to recognise all my loved ones in

Heaven, including my wife, despite the absence of marriage in Heaven.

These new bodies will be incorruptible. What a joy and relief to those like me who have suffered pain and limitation for years. No more decay or deterioration. Praise God! The hymn writer H.F. Lyte wrote in one of his hymns – 'change and decay in all around I see, O Thou who changest not, abide with me'. Everything on earth decays, including our bodies. Hearing, sight, mobility all deteriorate, but our new bodies never change or decay. I will be able to give my hearing aid to the nearest angel and say 'take it away, I will never need it again.' Hallelujah! *So will it be with the resurrection of the dead. The body that is sown is perishable, it is raised* **imperishable** (1 Corinthians 15:42). Our new bodies will not need hearing aids, crutches, walking sticks or medicines.

In Heaven we will be beautiful, strong, and glorious. We may not feel very beautiful down here. Try as we might, our wrinkles do not disappear. My own battered twisted face is not very beautiful. Even if we put on make-up with a trowel people 'see through it!' We may not feel very strong for our strength diminishes. Once I could carry two 112 pound bags of cement, but these days a bag of potatoes is more like it! The Scripture describes things well – *it* (the body) *is sown in dishonour, it is raised in glory; it is sown in* **weakness**, *it is raised in* **power** ... *it is sown a* **natural body**, *it is raised a* **spiritual body** (1 Corinthians 15:43, 44). Scripture promises us that we shall be beautiful, strong and glorious, because it says *Dear friends, now we are children of God, and what we will be has not yet been made known. But we know that when he appears,* **we shall be like him**, *for we shall see him as he is* (1 John 3:2).

Will we know each other there?

I believe that we will remember and recognise each other, even though we have our new bodies by then. In Scripture Jesus spoke about a man who had died, yet he recognised

Abraham, and also remembered his own brothers. It was an **actual** event which Jesus saw – it was not a parable, if it was, He would have said so. *There **was** a rich man who was dressed in purple and fine linen and lived in luxury every day. At his gate was laid a beggar named Lazarus, covered with sores and longing to eat what fell from the rich man's table. Even the dogs came and licked his sores. The time came when the beggar died and the **angels** carried him to Abraham's side. The rich man also died and was buried. In hell, where he was in torment, he looked up and **saw Abraham** far away, with Lazarus by his side* (Luke 16:19–23). In Hades (a realm beyond the grave) Lazarus, and Abraham all recognised each other. I cannot see that Christians will not know each other in Heaven. On another occasion Jesus heard that His friend had died, but when He called out to Lazarus to come out of the grave where he had been for four days, Lazarus heard Him. Lazarus was still Lazarus even though he was in the hereafter. By the way, it was wise of Jesus to only call Lazarus, otherwise all the dead would have risen! Jesus said that at the Judgement other specifically named people would be there – *The **men of Nineveh** will stand up at the judgment with this generation and condemn it; for they repented at the preaching of Jonah, and now one greater than Jonah is here. The **Queen of the South** (Queen of Sheba) will rise at the judgment with this generation and condemn it; for she came from the ends of the earth to listen to Solomon's wisdom, and now one greater than Solomon is here* (Matthew 12:41–42). Jesus said about the woman who anointed His feet with perfume that her act would be recorded forever. *When she poured this perfume on my body, she did it to prepare me for burial. I tell you the truth, wherever this gospel is preached throughout the world, what she has done will also be told, in memory of her* (Matthew 26:12–13). She was specifically mentioned. Surely then God intended her to be known in Heaven! So I believe that there is recognition in the supernatural realm.

Another reason why we will know each other in Heaven is the fact that God created us as individuals. On earth we have unique characteristics such as fingerprints, DNA, and even an individual body odour. In fact there is now a gadget which recognises this odour and identifies the owner of it. It is so accurate that some firms use the individual body odour device to unlock the doors at the workplace. Incidentally the device does not distinguish male from female! If God has built in so many individual characteristics to each person on earth, why should He suddenly scrap His wonderful design? He seems to delight in individuality and it seems to be important to Him. Therefore I believe that He will ensure that we retain our individuality in Heaven. Our new body will not destroy our personal characteristics, it will enhance them!

At the Transfiguration, the disciples clearly recognised Moses and Elijah – *There he was transfigured before them. His face shone like the sun, and his clothes became as white as the light. Just then there appeared before them **Moses** and **Elijah**, talking with Jesus* (Matthew 17:2, 3). Remember that they were in the eternal state, so, in the eternal state of Heaven there is recognition. Here on earth God knows our names. Of course He does – can He miss anything? More wonderful still is the fact that He has them recorded in Heaven – *I will never blot out **his name** from the **book of life**, but **will acknowledge his name** before my Father and his angels* (Revelation 3:5). *If anyone's **name** was not found written in the book of life, he was thrown into the lake of fire* (Revelation 20:15). Jesus knew my name when He died for me; He knows my name now, and regards me as an individual; my name is in His book of life. It is likely that Alexander will be my name forever.

Therefore, those who know me now will know me then. The only verse which may contradict me is – ... *I will also give him a white stone with a new name written on it, known only to him who receives it* (Revelation 2:17). But I will know when I get there! Our desire to be with, and to recognise each other is natural, and I believe that our desire will be fulfilled. However, the main thing is to see and be with Christ. **He** will be the focus of our attention.

Perhaps another reason for believing that we will know each other in Heaven is that, because we are all in the family of God, we will all have the family likeness. Even on earth we recognise fellow Christians fairly easily. Let me pile up the Scriptures that refer to us as the family of God – *Yet to all who received him, to those who believed in his name, he gave the right to become **children of God** (John 1:12). The Spirit himself testifies with our spirit that we are God's children (Romans 8:16). Consequently, you are no longer foreigners and aliens, but fellow citizens with God's people and members of **God's household** (Ephesians 2:19). So, although there are no sexual relationships in Heaven, we are still God's family there. Even on earth families know each other, so why shouldn't we know each other in Heaven? On earth no two people are exactly alike. They have a unique identity, so why should it be different in Heaven?

What about married partners?

We are not subject to death in Heaven, therefore we do not need to reproduce in order to perpetuate life. So, the marriage relationship will cease. We will be asexual like the angels who do not marry. *At the resurrection people will neither marry nor be given in marriage; they will be like the **angels** in Heaven* (Matthew 22:30). However, there is no suggestion in the Bible that a woman will not retain her distinctiveness as a woman. It simply says that there is no marriage. So, we will not be separated from our partners because a Christian man's wife is also his sister in the Lord. We have this dual relationship while we are on the earth, but in Heaven, the relationship will continue on the basis that we are all children of God, therefore 'related', and always together there. If someone had more than one spouse on earth, or if those who were widowed married again, there will be no problem because there is no marriage there. Nor will there be the resentment which may have caused a divorce on earth.

The joy of reunion, and introduction

I have a long list of those I want meet again, including my parents, and my 'spiritual parents'. Then I want to meet those of whom I have only heard or read. Elijah, Moses, Hosea, Obadiah, and so on. (By the way, I have made sure that I have read their books. I don't want to look foolish when they ask me if I enjoyed their writings!) I want to meet Mnason because I am interested as to why he was only mentioned once in the Bible. I want to see if Solomon is there, and Daniel and Nebuchadnezzar. It will be fun if those two meet again! Will Ananias and Sapphira be there? They might be, for we should never underestimate God's grace even though He causes some to die prematurely for their sinful conduct. Enoch will be able to tell us what it was like to walk with God and never die. Mary, Jesus' earthly mother will be there and will doubtless testify to Jesus' godliness while a child. Job will laugh out loud as he realises how completely God used him to confound the devil. Jeremiah will not be the weeping prophet in Heaven, but a cheerful, well rewarded man. Gladys Aylward will be far more than a housemaid in Heaven – she will wear a crown. So, get busy; start thinking about the fellowship we are going to enjoy with so many recognisable people.

Everything in Heaven is beautiful

Think of the most beautiful view you have ever seen on earth – the scenery in Heaven is better. Think of the loveliest music you have ever heard – the music in Heaven will surpass it. Recall the most beautiful person you have ever met – all those in Heaven will eclipse them and that without wrinkle cream! Let us consider some of the beautiful things in Heaven.

Beautiful materials

Here on earth people, especially women, use jewels for adornment. They like the play of light on their earrings and necklaces as they move their heads. Large sums of money are gladly paid for fine cut diamonds (not mentioned in the list in Revelation!). Consider these beautiful things mentioned in Scripture – gold, and gems of all descriptions. The play of light on them which would put the most fabulous jeweller's window display to shame. *Then I saw a new Heaven and a new earth, for the first Heaven and the first earth had passed away, and there was no longer any sea* (Revelation 21:1). *The construction of its wall was of jasper; and the city was pure gold, like clear glass. The foundations of the wall of the city were adorned with all kinds of precious stones: the first foundation was jasper, the second sapphire, the third chalcedony, the fourth emerald, the fifth sardonyx, the sixth sardius, the seventh chrysolite, the eighth beryl, the ninth topaz, the tenth chrysoprase, the eleventh jacinth, and the twelfth amethyst. The twelve gates were twelve pearls: each individual gate was of one pearl. And the street of the city was pure gold, like transparent glass* (Revelation 21:18–21 NKJV). I believe that these gems are actual gems, for I cannot see how they can be spiritualised.

We are used to buildings which are built with bricks, timber, or stone. Some of them are beautiful, and they reflect a degree of light. Those who have seen the walls and buildings of Jerusalem in the sunlight or even better at sunset will know how beautiful buildings can be. In Heaven these beautiful stones mentioned above are used for building materials! The buildings are made of gems which would bring far more than a kings ransom. I may be accused of being too literal here, but I will take the risk. After all, God made all precious stones, why shouldn't He use them? What alternatives would you suggest for such a 'City'?

Light – God's paintbrush

Even the finest gems need light to reflect from their facets, or to fluoresce. I used to work in a laboratory where they analysed minerals. On one occasion I was holding a piece of drab looking mineral in my hand while I was adjacent to ultra violet light. As the mineral came into contact with the light it emitted a beautiful radiance. It needed the right light – Heaven's light! All the gems in Heaven mentioned above give out beautiful rays because they are in the right light.

It is always light in Heaven, because God is light, therefore, wherever He is it is light. *The city does not need the sun or the moon to shine on it, for the glory of God gives it light, and the Lamb is its lamp. The nations will walk by its light, and the kings of the earth will bring their splendour into it.* **So it will never be dark in Heaven**. The beauty and brilliance of light there will never end. *On no day will its gates ever be shut, for there will be no night there* (Revelation 21:23–25). No darkness. Of course not – *This is the message we have heard from him and declare to you: God is light; in him there is no darkness at all* (1 John 1:5). That is the reason why *there will be* **no night there**. What a contrast to the dark, dirty, ugly aspects of this present world. I write a little more about the absence of darkness in chapter 14 – 'The Kingdom'.

Glorified people

Not only is Heaven a glorious place full of beauty, jewels, and light – its people are similar. In other words they are glorious people – glorified people. They are beautified with salvation, as I wrote in chapter 10 – 'The Wedding of Christ'. They are precious as gems, *'They shall be Mine,' says the LORD of hosts, 'On the day that I make them My jewels'* (Malachi 3:17 NKJV). They reflect the light of God – *Then the righteous will shine like the sun in the kingdom of their Father. He who has ears, let him hear* (Matthew 13:43).

As Christians we will be glorified in Heaven. But we will not have the basic, intrinsic glory which belongs to God alone. Being glorified does not mean that we will be so exactly like God that we could replace Him. He has said that ... *I will not yield my glory to another* (Isaiah 48:11). How then can we be glorified in Heaven? Firstly, Scripture **says** that we will be glorified. *And those he predestined, he also called; those he called, he also justified; those he* *justified, he also **glorified*** (Romans 8:30). But if we look at the word 'glorified' we find that it can mean honoured and exalted. I want to use the words 'honoured' and 'exalted' to describe our glorification, which happens partly on earth and mainly in Heaven.

God honours us on earth

As we serve Him here, He honours us here. . . . *Those who honour me I will honour* . . . (1 Samuel 2:30).

He honours us by choosing us

Peter, an apostle of Jesus Christ, To God's elect, . . . who have been chosen according to the foreknowledge of God the Father, through the sanctifying work of the Spirit, for obedience to Jesus Christ and sprinkling by his blood (1 Peter 1:1–2). We are honoured by having been given God's life, His nature, His Name and His Image.

He honours us by giving us such a calling

Think what that calling is – we are priests, intercessors, ambassadors representing Him on the earth, warriors, and stewards of the Gospel. I sometimes get overwhelmed by the sheer nobility of our calling whether on earth or in Heaven. I hope you do!

We have the honour of reflecting His glory

Reflecting it to others by the life we live, and by letting our light shine. It will shine as we make time to gaze at God; the Bible says so. *And we, who with unveiled faces all **reflect the Lord's glory**, are being transformed into his likeness with ever-increasing glory, which comes from the Lord, who is the Spirit* (2 Corinthians 3:18). What a thrill! Let us reflect it even more down here as Jesus commanded us – *let your light shine before men, that they may see your good deeds and praise your Father in Heaven* (Matthew 5:16). The more time we spend meditating upon (or looking at) Him, the more we glorify Him on earth.

How beautifully this is put in a verse of John Newton's hymn –

> 'When we've been there a thousand years,
> **Bright shining** as the sun,
> I've no less days to sing God's praise
> Than when I first begun.'

*Those who are wise **will** shine like the brightness of the Heavens, and those who lead many to righteousness, like the stars for ever and ever* (Daniel 12:3). When we walk in the light of Heaven we will be radiating the light of God in a most splendid fashion.

We will be glorified and exalted in the sense that we will have the honour of reflecting Him all the time without sin spoiling our reflecting. The Bible supports this – *everyone who is called by my name, whom I created for **my glory**, whom I formed and made* (Isaiah 43:7). *When Christ, who is your life, appears, then you also will appear with him in **glory*** (Colossians 3:4).

God exalts us in Heaven

We are greatly honoured and exalted by our position on earth, but we will be **fully** honoured and exalted in Heaven. We, like Jesus, will not be **fully** glorified (honoured, esteemed, magnified) until we are in Glory. Something remains to be completed on a future occasion. As always Jesus is our example. When He was on the earth He glorified God by the life He lived, therefore in return God honoured what He did and said. When He prayed *Father, glorify your name!* God answered Him, *I have **glorified** it, and will glorify it again* (John 12:28). And yet He was not **fully** glorified until He rose again and returned to Heaven as the Bible says: ... *God, who raised him from the dead and **glorified** him* (1 Peter 1:21); ... *Up to that time the Spirit had not been given, since Jesus had **not yet been glorified*** (John 7:39), i.e. on His return to Heaven. Jesus is glorified now and He together with us is looking forward to ***the day he*** *comes to be **glorified** in his holy people and to be marvelled at among all those who have believed* (2 Thessalonians 1:10). What a prospect – what an honour!

We are heirs of God already, but our **full** inheritance is reserved in Heaven for us. Peter tells us that we have been honoured with an inheritance – *and into an inheritance that can never perish, spoil or fade – **kept in heaven for you*** (1 Peter 1:4).

Not only are we beautiful, noble, majestic people like Jesus, we are also honoured heirs. In the East an heir was a very honoured person, and was dressed in the finest clothes, and he walked about with an air of authority. We shall be similar, but even grander because we are the heirs of Heaven. . . . *heirs – heirs of God and **co-heirs** with Christ, if indeed we share in his sufferings in order that we may also share in his glory* (Romans 8:17). Because of His grace we are given a place there as an **inheritance** as it says in the Bible – *He who overcomes will **inherit** all this, and I will be his God and he will be my son* (Revelation 21:7). If we are *heirs of God*, what is there that will not be ours in Heaven? Does earth belong to God? Do the stars belong to Him? Do the far reaches of space belong to Him? If the answer to these questions is 'yes' then all these will be ours too. This is not a figment of the imagination – the Bible declares it. Rumour has it that my father was swindled out of his large inheritance many years ago. If it is true, then it is a pity, but, because he was a Christian, he has a place which can never be taken away from him. (See you there Dad.) Apparently millions of pounds were involved, but in the light of his Heavenly inheritance how small this one was. Not only will we have an inheritance in Heaven, but it will be an unspoiled inheritance – *and into an inheritance that can **never perish, spoil or fade** – kept in Heaven for you* (1 Peter 1:4). We are indeed honoured, rich people in Heaven.

As heirs we have an exalted position in Heaven. Consider what the Bible says about us: *But there is a place where someone has testified: 'What is man that you are mindful of him, the son of man that you care for him? You made him a* *little lower than the angels; you **crowned him** with glory and honour and **put everything under his feet**.'* In putting every-thing under him, God left nothing that is not subject to him. *Yet at present we do not see everything subject to him* (Hebrews 2:6–8). The word 'crowns' means dignifies, beau-tifies. It signifies those who are exalted and honoured. This Scripture is not referring to God as I used to think, but it is referring to **man**! How God has exalted us! I write more about our exalted position in chapter 14 – 'The Kingdom'.

Nothing will ever spoil Heaven

Heaven is unspoiled, for God is there, and nothing can enter His Home which would spoil it because there are only beau-tiful things in it. We will see God – we will be like God. How could anything or anyone spoil it? At the moment the earth is spoiled because of the evil in it. It has been plundered, misused, and neglected We have been very bad stewards of it. There is a total absence of evil in Heaven, as there will be on earth when Jesus reigns. The earth was cursed because of sin. Thorns and thistles, weeds and decay came to it after the Fall. But in Heaven there will be no sign of the curse.

No tears or grief in Heaven

Tears, death, and pain were brought in by the evil one, but these will be unknown in Heaven for there will never be anything to cause them. *He will wipe every tear from their eyes. There will be no more death or mourning or crying or pain, for the old order of things has passed away* (Revelation 21:4). Although there is no grief in Heaven, some people ask the question – 'Will we be able to see our unsaved loved ones in Hell from Heaven, for if we can, we will surely have to grieve over them?' This is impossible in the final Heaven because there will not be anything to spoil it, and grieving would do exactly that. But even if we could see our unsaved loved ones, we would not grieve because grief is an imper-fect emotion which is absent in Heaven. Let me quote again a key verse – *Nothing impure* (imperfect, such as grief) *will ever enter it, nor will anyone who does what is shameful or deceitful, but only those whose names are written in the Lamb's book of life* (Revelation 21:27). Instead of grieving we will see how perfect God's justice was and is, and we will praise the *God of all the earth for doing right.* He gave them the choice, but they chose Hell. So God confirmed what they wanted, and we will be satisfied with this, and untroubled by the fate of the ungodly. As for us, we will be busy serving God – ... *The throne of God and of the Lamb will be in the city, and his servants will serve him* (Revelation 22:3). No wonder that Christians have always looked forward to this wonderful, unspoilt, joyous, eternal Home which is prepared for them. They were looking forward to it in Bible times; they still are today – *But in keeping with his promise we are looking forward to a new Heaven and a new earth, the home of righteousness* (2 Peter 3:13). Of course, those who look forward to it get ready for it. I hope you are!

Time in Heaven

Time in Heaven will not exist as we know it here. On earth it is a blessing in that it gives us opportunities to use it. It is also a frustration because it limits us. I write more about it in chapter 14 – 'The Kingdom'.

We will be rewarded in Heaven

Read about this in chapter 11 – 'The Judgement Seat of Christ'.

Will we all be equal in Heaven?

As to salvation, we will all be equal, because we are all children of God. There will be no favouritism. Scripture stresses this – *For God does not show favouritism* (Romans

2:11); *Then Peter began to speak: 'I now realise how true it is that God does not show favouritism'* (Acts 10:34). We are all known to God as individuals, and His love to us is the same as His love to every other person in Heaven. If it is true that some will have a greater position in Heaven, there will be no jealousy or resentment, for these emotions are entirely absent from God's home, because they are absent from His heart, and will be from ours.

However, God is faithful to His servants who have laboured extra long and hard on the earth, and Scripture does seem to indicate different positions for some in Heaven. Not that God regards them as of more worth than others, but that they are more qualified than others who have not been as diligent on earth. There seem to be different positions in Heaven. *Jesus said to them, '... to sit at my right or left is not for me to grant. **These places belong to those for whom they have been prepared** by my Father'* (Matthew 20:23). And again – *'Well done, my good servant!' his master replied. 'Because you have been trustworthy in a very small matter, **take charge of ten cities**'* (Luke 19:17).

Let the Scripture spur us on to be more diligent and faithful while we have the chance. Then God may entrust us with greater things in Heaven. *Remember this: Whoever sows sparingly will also reap sparingly, and whoever sows generously will also reap generously* (2 Corinthians 9:6).

I write more about this in chapter 11 – 'The Judgement Seat of Christ'.

✠ ✠ ✠

Common questions about Heaven

There are Christians who miss their departed loved ones so much, that they long to make some kind of contact with them. So they ask, 'Can those who have gone before us, see us?' There are no Scriptures which tell us definitely that those who have preceded us can see us. People may feel that their loved ones are watching over them, and even praying for them, but there is no Scripture to back this up, and, although I understand their desire to feel close to their loved ones, it is not a biblical concept and therefore must be abandoned.

Some sincere Christians from a Roman Catholic background asked me the question 'Do the departed saints pray for us?' My answer was that the term 'saints' in Scripture simply means 'true believers, or holy ones'. In other words, those who are born again. *To all ... who are loved by God and called to be **saints**: Grace and peace to you from God our Father and from the Lord Jesus Christ* (Romans 1:7). The Roman Catholic idea of saints as dead people who have a special access to God is quite unscriptural. Scripture makes it plain that only Jesus mediates for us. *For there is one God and one mediator between God and men, the man Christ Jesus* (1 Timothy 2:5).

Who are the 'great cloud of witnesses'?

There is a popular notion that in Heaven we have a great crowd of departed Christians cheering us on in our life down here. Indeed some preachers use a verse to back up the idea. *Therefore, since we are surrounded by such a great cloud of witnesses, let us throw off everything that hinders and the sin that so easily entangles, and let us run with perseverance the race marked out for us* (Hebrews 12:1). However, these witnesses (martyrs) are those who were witnesses (living testimonies, martyrs) **in their own generation**. The word 'witness' implies one who testifies to something, more than one who observes (sees) something, and they are only examples to us today. The verse does not say that they are watching us. And it certainly does not say that they pray for us. The writer of Hebrews is using the example of the faith, courage, and perseverance of the *cloud of witnesss* to urge us on to do the same in our Christian life down here. He is **not** teaching that these departed people are actually witnessing or watching us.

Can we contact the dead?

Trying to contact the dead, whether they are saved or unsaved, is expressly forbidden in Scripture. *Let no one be found among you who sacrifices his son or daughter in the fire, who practises divination or sorcery, interprets omens, engages in witchcraft, or casts spells, or who is a medium or spiritist or who consults the dead* (Deuteronomy 18:10–11). There is the incident in Scripture where two men from Heaven joined Jesus and some disciples. *Two men, Moses and Elijah, appeared in glorious splendour, talking with Jesus. They spoke about his departure, which he was about to bring to fulfilment at Jerusalem* (Luke 9:31). But this was a special case, and we should not think otherwise. Anyway, they were not in Heaven then, but on earth. If God wants anything communicated from Heaven, He will do it through the Holy Spirit; the Bible; or through angels, but never through those who are dead. As for anyone in Heaven **wanting** to contact us; I cannot imagine that they would, because they would be totally absorbed in God. Absorbed eternally as in the next chapter . . .

Chapter 6

Our Life in Heaven is Eternal

Whenever I write about Heaven, or preach on it, I find a greater longing to be there. The joy and the thrill of it are meat and drink to me. Having written in the last chapter about its joys I simply add another simple but wonderful fact about Heaven – it lasts forever! Jesus wants us to know this, so He said to His disciples, which includes us (for all true Christians are disciples), *I give them **eternal** life, and they shall **never perish**; no-one can snatch them out of my hand* (John 10:28). As if that is not enough, God repeats in other verses: *And this is the testimony: God has given us eternal life, and this life is in his Son. I write these things to you who believe in the name of the Son of God so that you may know that you have eternal life* (1 John 5:11, 13). God wants us to be very sure about it, and to get excited by it. Get excited now!

The term 'eternal life' can be frightening. That is if we only think of the **everlasting** aspect of it. It can seem as though we are stuck in a place that we may not like, and that there is no escape from it. But if we really love God, and we remember that He is there, we will not be afraid. It is far better to think of the **quality** of eternal life. It is indeed a continuous, endless existence, but it is also a **kind** of life which frees us from death and decay. It is endlessly satisfying, exciting, and joyful. Jesus did not only promise us life in Heaven, He promised us **abundant** life. He said, *I have* *come that they may have life, and have it **to the full*** (John 10:10).

Eternity is not just endless time, but a different realm, or mode of being. Derek Prince says:

> 'Time and space are inseparably related. Neither can be defined apart from the other in this age. In the eternal era, "space and time" as we know it now will cease to be. God will replace it with eternity; His mode of existence.'   (Foundation Series)

Eternal can only mean eternal

I have written about eternity in relation to the unsaved dead in chapter 23 – 'Hell is Eternal'. I deplore the attempts made to change the meaning of the word by the Annihilationists and others. If we meddle with the word eternal in connection with the unsaved dead, we must meddle with it in connection with the saved. And in connection with God Himself, who is described as the *eternal God*. We must beware of the danger of denying Scriptures such as the following which deal with eternal punishment, life, sin, salvation, judgement, redemption and covenant. I quote quite a few to show how dangerous it is to meddle with the word eternal.

*Then they will go away to **eternal punishment**, but the righteous to **eternal life*** (Matthew 25:46). *But whoever blasphemes against the Holy Spirit will never be forgiven; he is guilty of an **eternal sin*** (Mark 3:29). *And, once made perfect, he became the source of **eternal salvation** for all who obey him* (Hebrews 5:9). ... *instruction about baptisms, the laying on of hands, the resurrection of the dead, and **eternal judgment*** (Hebrews 6:2). *He did not enter by means of the blood of goats and calves; but he entered the Most Holy Place once for all by his own blood, having obtained **eternal redemption*** (Hebrews 9:12). *May the God of peace, who through the blood of the **eternal covenant** brought back from the dead our*

Lord Jesus, that great Shepherd of the sheep (Hebrews 13:20).

God is eternal

The most serious thing in such meddling is the fact that **God** is described as eternal. Are we going to throw doubt on that? The Bible certainly does not do so. It points out that God is eternal, everlasting and immortal. The fact that **we** also become eternal is due to the grace of God in imparting such life to us. His 'eternity' is intrinsic; ours is derived.

Consider some Scriptures about God being eternal –

*... but now revealed and made known through the prophetic writings by the command of the **eternal** God, so that all nations might believe and obey him* (Romans 16:26). *The **eternal** God is your refuge, and underneath are the everlasting arms* (Deuteronomy 33:27). *For since the creation of the world God's invisible qualities – his **eternal** power and divine nature – have been clearly seen, being understood from what has been made, so that men are without excuse* (Romans 1:20).

And some which use the linked words immortal and everlasting. Everlasting is synonymous with eternal, and the word 'immortal' (Greek: *athanasia) is deathlessness. God will never die!*

Do you not know? Have you not heard? The LORD *is the **everlasting God**, the Creator of the ends of the earth. He will not grow tired or weary, and his understanding no one can fathom* (Isaiah 40:28). *... who alone is **immortal** and who lives in unapproachable light, whom no one has seen or can see. To him be honour and might forever. Amen* (1 Timothy 6:16). *Now to the King eternal, **immortal**, invisible, the only God, be honour and glory for ever and ever. Amen* (1 Timothy 1:17).

All through the ages men and women have looked for eternal existence or immortality. Most of the world's religions teach that man will live on after death in some form or another. Consider the Egyptians loading their kings tombs with provisions for the after-life. Or the people in the Bible looking for immortality, although their views differed drastically from the heathen ideas. Job said, *I know that my Redeemer lives, and that in the end he will stand upon the earth. And after my skin has been destroyed, yet in my flesh I will* **see God** (Job 19:25, 26).

David said, *because you will not abandon me to the grave, nor will you let your Holy One see decay* (Psalm 16:10); *You guide me with your counsel, and afterward you will take me into glory* (Psalm 73:24). Paul said, *Now we know that if the earthly tent we live in is destroyed, we have a building from God, an eternal house in heaven, not built by human hands* (2 Corinthians 5:1). This is the Christian's understanding of eternal life. Because God is eternal, He can never change. He says so through the prophet. *I the LORD do not change. So you, O descendants of Jacob, are not destroyed* (Malachi 3:6). What a relief to know someone who is **always** the same, and with whom we always know where we are. He will always be loving, therefore we need never doubt His love. He will always tell the truth, therefore we can always depend on what He has said. He will always be merciful, therefore we can always find mercy.

Several points of view about 'eternal'

Traditional view

Those who hold this view say that man was created an eternal being and therefore all who are born inherit this ever-existing quality. Some Traditionalists cite the Scripture to prove it – *He has also* **set eternity in the hearts** *of men* (Ecclesiastes 3:11). Other verses cited by Traditionalists to prove that man is born eternal are: *So God created man in his own image, in the* **image of God** *he created him; male and female he created them* (Genesis 1:27); *the LORD God formed the man from the dust of the ground and breathed into his nostrils the breath of life, and the man became a* **living** *being* (Genesis 2:7). Their inference is that God breathed His life into man, and made the spirit of man 'ever-existing' because

God is eternal. He impressed His own eternal Image upon man. But He did not impart His **deity** to man.

As for immortality, Traditionalists say that man was immortal (his spirit was deathless) before the Fall, because the seeds of decay and death were not in him. They say that because sin came in at the Fall, all mankind became subject to **physical** death and judgement, quoting *The soul who sins is the one who will die* (Ezekiel 18:20), and *Just as man is destined to die once, and after that to face judgment* (Hebrews 9:27).

My own view is that we were created by God as eternal beings, and that our spirit cannot die. I believe that we have the potential as born again Christians for immortality, although strictly speaking, we only become **actually** immortal when we are resurrected.

The Conditional Immortality view

Those who preach this doctrine believe that man becomes immortal or eternal, only when he is born anew, and is resurrected. Man is, of course, still subject to **physical** death while he is on earth. *To those who by persistence in doing good seek glory, honour and immortality, he will give* (e.g. it is future) *eternal life* (Romans 2:7). *So will it be with the resurrection of the dead. The body that is sown is perishable, it is raised imperishable* (incorruptible) (1 Corinthians 15:42). Some of those who hold this doctrine say that the unsaved are not immortal, but at death, they are punished proportionally for a time, then they pass into non-existence, therefore suffering the loss of God and Heaven forever.

The Annihilation view

I deal with annihilation more fully in the Hell/Arguments section.

Eternal life? Or eternal existence?

There is a difference between mere **existence** and real **living**. On earth a man who is blind, deaf, and paralysed can

hardly be said to **live**. He is alive, but not fulfilled. I speak
from personal experience, for I was blind, deaf, and paralysed for a while! In Heaven the saved **live** forever. They **live**
as opposed to existing. The saved are in **life** – as opposed to
mere **existence**. God *made us **alive with Christ** even when we
were dead in transgressions – it is by grace you have been
saved* (Ephesians 2:5). Jesus brought us into the greatest life
imaginable when He rose victorious from the grave. He
says to us today, *Because I live, you also will **live*** (John
14:19). *The thief comes only to steal and kill and destroy; I
have come that they may have life, and have it **to the full***
(John 10:10). To enjoy full (the KJV uses the word 'abundant') life, we need stimulation. God is such a stimulating
Person. I can imagine Him when we been in Heaven for ten
thousand years, saying to us 'have you enjoyed what you
have seen?' When we say 'yes Lord, it's great', He will probably say 'I am glad, but come and see this new thing,
another dimension of this great Home.' I can imagine this
being repeated for ever. There will be so much to do, to
explore, to enjoy. It will be so stimulating and enjoyable.

The saved receive the **right** to eternal life here and now.
We are living in the joyful expectation of this abundant life
here and now, on the earth. It is a wonderful foretaste of
what is to come in Heaven. We have the right to eternal life
when we are born again. God says, *Yet to all who received
him, to those who believed in his name, he gave the right to
become children of God* (John 1:12). *But if Christ is in you,
your body is dead because of sin, yet your spirit is alive
because of righteousness* (Romans 8:10). At our new birth
the Spirit of God came into our lives. *And if the Spirit of
him who raised Jesus from the dead is living in you, he who
raised Christ from the dead will also give life to your mortal
bodies through his Spirit, who lives in you* (Romans 8:11).
The Holy Spirit is the Agent of the Godhead, and He
brought to us the new life which Jesus obtained for us
through the sacrifice of Calvary. *And this is the testimony:
God has given us eternal life, and this life is in his Son. He
who has the Son has life; he who does not have the Son of*

God does not have life (1 John 5:11, 12). God wants us to know the joy of eternal life now. He wants to fill our hearts with assurance and expectation of even better things to come. As someone wrote, 'grace is glory begun'. God loves to assure us about eternal life – *I write these things to you who believe in the name of the Son of God so that you **may** know that you have eternal life* (1 John 5:13).

It is at the Resurrection that we will **actually** receive **completed** immortality, and **eternal** salvation. The saved suffer physical death because of the Fall as the unsaved do because the present body is not deathless even though the spirit is alive because of regeneration. They are alive to God – because the barriers are destroyed – and they are reconciled to God. But at the Resurrection, they actually **receive** their new body which makes them **actually** immortal (deathless). Therefore, in Heaven they are forever in **life** because they are forever with God who is life. They also have their new body which is deathless. I write more about this in chapter 8 – 'There will be a Resurrection'.

The unsaved only *exist* forever

Eternal death (endless existence in a useless state) is the lot of the unsaved. It was our lot until we were saved. *As for you, you **were** dead in your transgressions and sins* (Ephesians 2:1). The unsaved suffered physical death because of the Fall. Now, in addition, they suffer the death of separation from God, who is **life**. They are resurrected, but with their old body. This is dealt with more fully in chapter 23 – 'Hell is Eternal'.

Having written about what Heaven is like, and the joy of eternity, let us now consider how we actually get there. The transfer from this life to the next life. The next chapter describes the start.

Chapter 7

Death

The way from here to Heaven passes through death for all of us. Death is not nice, but it is only like a curtain through which we brush into the eternal life which I have just written about. The **process** of death is not always a nice one, but God can enable us to cope with it. In this chapter I am dealing with death as it affects a Christian. I deal with death for the unsaved in chapter 19 – 'Death and Resurrection for the Lost'.

Life here is brief

There may be times when we wonder just how much more trouble we can take in our daily life. Our cares and problems may seem endless, and make us wonder how much longer they will go on for. But life is brief really, and there are many reminders of this. Our children are not small for long; they grow up quickly and leave home in no time. We go to work year after year, and old age seems a long way away, but it comes surprisingly quickly. The Bible sums up life's brevity well – ... *What is your life? You are a mist that appears for a little while and then vanishes* (James 4:14). *The length of our days is seventy years – or eighty, if we have the strength; yet their span is but trouble and sorrow, for they quickly pass, and we fly away* (Psalm 90:10). My wife and I used to have a saying when we had to decorate the house, or do something rather big to it. We used to say 'let's put it on the 35 year plan.' Later on in our life we would talk about the 10 year plan. Now we are wary about using the term 'year' at all! Life goes by so quickly. Anyway, the main purpose in life down here is as an apprenticeship for Heaven. Seventy years is quite a short preparation for everlasting life!

Death comes to us all, and no one escapes it. The only exceptions to this statement are the Christians who are alive at the Second Coming of Jesus. They will not die, but be caught up with those Christians who have died but who are resurrected at the same time. Some of the unsaved people have put their trust in scientific techniques (cryogenics) and had their bodies 'put on ice' in order to escape death. But they are no match for the God who has made irrevocable decrees. The Psalmist said, *What man can live and not see death, or save himself from the power of the grave? Selah* (Psalm 89:48). The answer is – **no one**. The Bible deals with facts, and the fact is that there is *a time to be born and a time to die, a time to plant and a time to uproot* (Ecclesiastes 3:2). All will die, so let all be ready to die.

There are three meanings of 'death'

1. Separation of the spirit from the body

This refers to physical death when the spirit and the body part company. Paul speaks of it when he saw that the moment of his death was near – *because I know that I will soon put it* (the body) *aside, as our Lord Jesus Christ has made clear to me* (2 Peter 1:14). And again – *Just as man is destined to die once, and after that to face judgement* (Hebrews 9:27).

2. Separation of the spirit from God

This is the condition of those who are physically alive on earth, but not alive to God, i.e. they are not in touch with Him, nor do they have His new life within them because they are not born again. It is a dreadful condition to be in.

I was in it once, and the Bible describes it. *Remember that at that time you were separate from Christ, excluded from citizenship in Israel and foreigners to the covenants of the promise,* **without hope** *and without God in the world* (Ephesians 2:12). Christians, before they were born again were – **dead** *in your transgressions and sins* (Ephesians 2:1). This is obviously not physical death for Paul is writing to those who were physically alive. How wonderful it is that Christians can say – He made us alive with Christ even when we were dead in transgressions – it is by grace you have been saved (Ephesians 2:5). God will perform this miracle for anyone who will come and ask Him to do it for them. Do you need it?

3. Separation from God completely

This is the awful, final state in which the unsaved are when they have died physically, been raised at the resurrection, and been judged by God. It is the death referred to in Scripture – *The soul who sins is the one who will die* (eternally) . . . (Ezekiel 18:20), and described again in another verse as . . . *the second death* (Revelation 20:14).

The cause of death

Death both physical and spiritual, is a result of sin coming into the world, and a punishment for it. If only Adam and Eve had been more careful! If only they had obeyed God's command – *but you must not eat from the tree of the knowledge of good and evil, for when you eat of it you will surely die* (Genesis 2:17). Tragically they did disobey God, and death came into the world, both physical death, and spiritual death.

So God uttered His just verdict – *The soul who sins is the one who will* **die** (Ezekiel 18:4). God repeated it in New Testament times through Paul's words: . . . **death came to all men**, *because all sinned* (Romans 5:12); *For the wages of sin is* **death** (Romans 6:23). God's verdict cannot be contradicted. To do so we would have to be stronger than He is.

Where is such a person? This great God has clearly stated that – ... *I am the first and I am the last; apart from me there is no God* (Isaiah 44:6). Satan, who is more powerful than any man tried to contradict God but he utterly failed. What hope has any man to contradict God!

But – Christians do not fear death

It might be more true to say that Christians **need** not fear death. Sadly, many do fear it, but they need not do so. The reason why Christians need not fear death or dying is that death is defeated. God says in His Word that its power is destroyed – *The last enemy to be destroyed is death* (1 Corinthians 15:26); *Death has been swallowed up in victory. Where, O death, is your victory? Where, O death, is your sting?* (1 Corinthians 15:54b, 55).

Death once reigned supreme, but not now, because Jesus has died and risen again. ... *Christ Jesus, who has **destroyed** death and has brought life and immortality to light through the gospel* (2 Timothy 1:10). I sometimes think of Him standing outside the empty tomb, His foot firmly upon the neck of His enemies, His face aglow with triumph and exhilaration. Shouting aloud, 'I have done it, I have destroyed the enemy, once and for all.' If Jesus does not return in my lifetime, then I will die, but death will never hold me; it cannot, because God has delivered me from its imprisonment. Jesus, the Son of God did it once and for all. *Since the children have flesh and blood, he too shared in their humanity so that by his death he might destroy him who holds the power of death – that is, the devil – and free those who all their lives were held in slavery by their fear of death* (Hebrews 2:14–15). Jesus robbed death of all its power – He destroyed it to set us free from its power, and from fearing it. We **can** be free from this fear of death or dying if we **want** to be. The fear is rooted in our unbelief. The Bible says: ... *God has said, 'Never will I leave you; never will I forsake you'* (Hebrews 13:5); *For I am convinced that neither death nor life, neither angels nor demons, neither the present nor the future, nor any powers,*

*neither height nor depth, nor anything else in all creation, will
be able to separate us from the love of God that is in Christ
Jesus our Lord* (Romans 8:38–39). So, at the moment of
death, what is there to be afraid of? God never loses sight of
us at any time, we are too precious to Him for that. If God is
around when we die (and He **is**), what is there to fear? Is
some sneaky demon going to snatch us out of the arms of
the Father just as we pass away? Will God fail to notice us
when we die, and will He somehow lose interest in us? A
look at the price he paid to save us will dispel all such
nonsense. Why not receive freedom from fear of death, or
fear of dying even now, while you read this chapter?

Christians should not fear dying. To some people it is the
process of dying which makes them afraid. One of the
devil's most successful weapons is what I call anticipatory
fear. We reason 'supposing I cannot bear the pain, or what
if I fail as a Christian while I am in pain?' Once, after studying the end times doctrines in the church where I grew up, I
said to the elders 'I am not sure that I could go through the
great Tribulation, supposing I fall away from God.' One of
them said 'Alex, when you get to the time of Tribulation,
God will give you tribulation grace, but not before, because
you don't need it till then.' Many Christians say that they
are not sure that they will be victorious when they come to
die. But the same rule applies. God offers us what we need
when we need it. *But he said to me, 'My grace is sufficient for
you, for my power is made perfect in weakness.' Therefore I
will boast all the more gladly about my weaknesses, so that
Christ's power may rest on me* (2 Corinthians 12:9). Shall we
believe it, and press on?

If we are deeply rooted in God's love as the Bible exhorts
us to be, then we need not fear the process of dying. Paul
speaks about . . . *being rooted and established in love* (Ephesians 3:17). This means being utterly convinced of His love,
so that fear departs. We will only be *rooted and grounded* if
we make the time to meditate on the verses until they are
deep down in our heart, but it can be done. Why not start
now? Fear can spoil the joy of our hope. So, whatever our

fear is, whether it is fear of death, dying, pain, bereavement, the future, Heaven, or eternity, let us deal with it. Why not do it now, by first confessing fear as a sin (the Bible says hundreds of times *fear not*, so it must be sin to be afraid), then ask forgiveness, and **receive** God's forgiveness. Then turn your back on fear and taking God's hand, press on. Finally, meditate on Heaven until it becomes real and precious.

When unsaved people are dying, it is easy to give way to the fear of upsetting them and therefore failing to speak to them about eternity. But God urges us to reach out to them with the truths of Heaven and Hell. Consider our responsibility to do so in the light of God's Word – *When I say to the wicked, 'O wicked man, you will surely die,' and you do not speak out to dissuade him from his ways, that wicked man will die for his sin, and I will hold you accountable for his blood* (Ezekiel 33:8). God is not afraid to convict people of sin, even when they are dying, but He cannot do so if we are weak and cowardly in our witnessing. Which is worse for the dying; embarrassment and shock down here, or terror at the Judgement Seat after death?

Where do Christians go when they die?

Some scholars say that it was only the Old Testament believers who went to Sheol/Hades until Jesus ascended (they went to the 'good' side of it; a temporary resting place till the final Heaven). But now He has risen, they are in Heaven, i.e. the place or state variously described as 'The Presence of the Lord', 'Paradise', or the 'final Heaven'. Other scholars say that all believers are still in Hades (place of departed spirits) till the resurrection. They are saved, but await His Coming in order to be in the final Heaven.

To my mind it does not matter too much what terms we use to describe where we go to when we die. 'Paradise', 'Abraham's Bosom', 'the Presence of the Lord', all seem to be simply different names for Heaven. Our earthly homes are called by different names; i.e. house, castle, residence, dwelling etc. Why shouldn't we use different names for Heaven! The main thing when we die is that we are in the Presence of the Lord whom we love, and Who welcomes us to His Presence. Wherever we are, Jesus will come for us. That is the important thing. If we die before Jesus returns, we go into the Presence of the Lord. This seems to be what we might call 'the present Heaven'. Although some theologians call it 'Paradise', quoting – *Jesus answered him, 'I tell you the truth, today you will be with me in **paradise**'* (Luke 23:43). Paul also used the term – (I) *was caught up to **Paradise**. He heard inexpressible things, things that man is not permitted to tell* (2 Corinthians 12:4). As for the length of time we are there – there is no reckoning of time in the passage of the spirit from earth and Heaven. So, the question is irrelevant.

Angels know where we go when we die. They serve God by looking after His people. When we die, or if we are alive at the Second Coming, angels will take us to God as part of their special task of serving, guarding, and caring for us. We have this wonderful truth portrayed in the Bible – *Are not all angels ministering spirits sent to serve those who will inherit salvation?* (Hebrews 1:14). They make sure that when we die we get to Heaven. This seems to be illustrated in Scripture – *The time came when the beggar died and the angels carried him to Abraham's side. The rich man also died and was buried* (Luke 16:22). These great angels enforce the decree of Jesus which He made when He said – *I give them eternal life, and they shall never perish; no one can snatch them out of my hand* (John 10:28). If we are alive when Jesus returns, His angels will be assisting Him in bringing us to His presence – *... See, the Lord is coming with thousands upon thousands of his holy ones* (Jude 1:14). They have an important job to do – *And he will send his angels with a loud trumpet call, and they will gather his elect from the four winds, from one end of the Heavens to the other* (Matthew 24:31). Also – *For the Son of Man is going to come in his Father's glory with his angels, and then he will reward each person according to what he has done* (Matthew 16:27). How exciting it will be when we rise to

meet Jesus, with vast companies of angels accompanying us.
So, whether we die or are alive at His Coming, angels will
make sure that all the people who are born again (holy
ones) are brought into His presence. No need to fear – we
will get to the right place!

We need to prepare for death

It is unkind to leave our affairs in a mess for others to sort
out. While we are well and strong, we may feel disinclined to
think about making a will, and making provision for our
loved ones, but it is wise to do so while we can. Those who
love their families will set their affairs in order. So, make a
will. Arrange your funeral. Write your last letters to your
loved ones. Get ready to 'change your address'. Real Chris-
tianity is practical, so this procedure is practical. After all,
death for Christians is not good-bye, but only 'until we meet
again', so there is nothing gloomy about these preparations.

God has made us emotional beings. He expects us to
grieve when our loved ones die. In His view it is normal to
grieve at such a time. Seeing that He has given us emotions
– how can it be wrong to vent them? The 'stiff upper lip'
attitude so common in the West has caused great harm to
those who accept it. Bottled up emotions can seriously
damage our health and our work for God. Let us learn to
grieve as they readily do in the East, and, by doing so,
maintain our emotional health.

Finally, let me ask you two questions. What are the first,
second, and third things that you will do when you get to
Heaven? Secondly, if you have a gravestone, what are you
going to have inscribed on it? At a conference, Peggy, my
wife asked the people this question and the answers were
interesting. One preacher suggested 'Gone to yet another
meeting'. Another said 'Hallelujah, I've made it'. Yet
another one was 'Now will you believe that I was ill?' What
are your last words to the world going to be? What does
death lead to? Heaven! But is there anything in between?
Yes – the Resurrection.

Chapter 8

There will be a Resurrection

The sequel to death is the Resurrection. The One who conquered death has ordained the Resurrection. But all through the centuries there have been some who have queried it. Many, like the Sadducees have denied that there is any such thing. Others favour the heresy of annihilation. But the Bible clearly states that there will be a Resurrection. *Do not be amazed at this, for a time is coming when **all** who are in their graves will hear his voice and come out – those who have done good will rise to live, and those who have done evil will rise to be condemned* (John 5:28–29). Paul points out that – *If there is no resurrection of the dead, then not even Christ has been raised. And if Christ has not been raised, our preaching is useless and so is your faith* (1 Corinthians 15:13, 14). No wonder that there are so many attacks on the Resurrection. What a way to discredit preaching about Jesus! But it won't work. Paul goes on to state – *But Christ **has** indeed been raised from the dead, the firstfruits of those who have fallen asleep* (1 Corinthians 15:20). This is the greatest proof that there is a resurrection – the fact that **Jesus** was resurrected from the dead. His resurrection is one of the best attested facts of history. Scripture makes it very plain – *that he was buried, that he was raised on the third day according to the Scriptures, and that he appeared to Peter, and then to the Twelve. After that, he appeared to more than five hundred of the brothers at the same time, most of whom are still living,* *though some have fallen asleep. Then he appeared to James, then to all the apostles, and last of all he appeared to me also, as to one abnormally born* (1 Corinthians 15:4–8). *After his suffering, he showed himself to these men and gave many convincing proofs that he was alive. He appeared to them over a period of forty days and spoke about the kingdom of God* (Acts 1:3).

No one can escape the resurrection. Whether we are buried, cremated, blown to bits, or die in our beds, we will be resurrected from the dead. God makes this plain through the vision that He gave to John – *And I saw the dead, **great and small**, standing before the throne, and books were opened. Another book was opened, which is the book of life. . . . The sea gave up the dead that were in it, and death and Hades gave up the dead that were in them* (Revelation 20:12–13). Some people wonder how a body which has been blown to bits can be put together again. God made our bodies in the first place, and He does not forget how we are made. So it is no problem for our Maker to reassemble the parts into a whole body again, and in the process to make them glorious and immortal. The method of our death is quite unimportant – the fact is that we shall rise again. The dead will hear God's voice, and when God issues a command, it is heard throughout Creation. He spoke before the foundation of the world and Creation appeared. All through Genesis chapters 1–3 we read the words of God – *let there be light – let the dry land appear – let the earth bring forth living creatures* (NKJV). The elements through which Creation was made heard God, and responded. In the Day of Resurrection, He will command all who have ever lived to come to His Throne. All the dead will hear His voice, and all will respond by standing before Him. Jesus made this plain when He said – *Do not be amazed at this, for a time is coming when all who are in their graves will **hear his voice*** (John 5:28). Jesus actually gave a prior demonstration of His ability to speak to the dead – *When he had said this, Jesus called in a loud voice, 'Lazarus, come out!'* (John 11:43). Lazarus was certainly dead; he stank after four days of death. But he heard God, and obeyed, just as all the dead will do on the day of Resurrection. It will not be possible for anyone to shut their ears to the sound. Whoever we are, wherever we are, we will rise from the dead. No one can hide from God, nor can they fail to hear His voice.

One resurrection, or two?

Scripture seems to me to indicate one resurrection, but with different aspects. Jesus refers to **the hour** in the KJV – *Marvel not at this: for **the hour** is coming, in the which all that are in the graves shall hear his voice* (John 5:28 KJV), or to **a time** in the NIV – *Do not be amazed at this, for **a time** is coming when all who are in their graves will hear his voice* (John 5:28). Both seem to refer to one Resurrection. Jesus also seems to indicate one Resurrection or Day in the following – *And this is the will of him who sent me, that I shall lose none of all that he has given me, but raise them up at **the** last day* (John 6:39). My feeling is that there is one resurrection, but with two aspects to it. The following verse indicates two aspects – *. . . and come out – those who have **done good** will rise to live, and those who have **done evil** will rise to be condemned* (John 5:29).

The first aspect is for the saved – for those whose names **are** written in God's Book of Life. These are the people raised from the dead to a place of absolute glory. Jesus made this possible by His atoning sacrifice at Calvary, and He was already looking forward to the Day of resurrection when He said to Mary and Martha – *I am the resurrection and the life. He who believes in me will live, even though he dies* (John 11:25). Never underestimate the joy and excitement in the heart of Jesus as He anticipates the Resurrection of His dear people. The Bible speaks of His satisfaction – *He shall see the labor of His soul, and **be satisfied**. . . . My righteous Servant shall justify many* (Isaiah 53:11 NKJV). *Justify many* sounds like the understatement of the age! There will be millions and millions of us responding to God's call. Abraham, Moses, Deborah, Mary, Paul, my grandmother, to name but a few. How many Christians do you know? Count them up, and look forward to being with them at the Resurrection.

The second aspect of the Resurrection is for the unsaved dead. Those whose names are not in the Book of Life. They will not be in Heaven, but will only see God at the Judgement Seat in the Heavenly place, or perhaps on earth, not in Heaven because – *Nothing impure will ever enter it, nor will anyone who does what is shameful or deceitful, but only those whose names are written in the Lamb's book of life* (Revelation 21:27). I have written more about this in chapter 19 – 'Death and Resurrection for the Lost'.

The Resurrection holds no fears for Christians

Just as we look forward to Heaven with great joy, so we look for the resurrection with joy and hope. It is part of our great hope, for how could we have the one without the other! Paul said it for all of us – *and I have the same hope in God as these men, that there will be a resurrection of both the righteous and the wicked* (Acts 24:15). David put it beautifully – *I shall see your face; when I awake, I will be satisfied with seeing your likeness* (Psalm 17:15). So, Christians need not fear the resurrection, nor the second death either – *He who has an ear, let him hear what the Spirit says to the churches. He who overcomes will not be hurt at all by the second death* (Revelation 2:11). As I said in chapter 7 – 'Death', death is the end of one era of our existence, and the resurrection is the beginning of our eternal life with God. Think about it, and begin to enjoy it already. Of course, as I have said, we may be alive when Jesus comes again. What a thrill if we are! So, let us look at the fact of His Coming, so that we can get ready for it in case He comes soon.

Chapter 9

The Second Coming

The second Coming of Jesus is often referred to as the Rapture. Some people say that it is the same event as the Day of the Lord in Scripture, although others disagree. With over three hundred references to His Coming, there are bound to be different understandings of it amongst equally godly people. After reading the Scriptures for ourselves we must, as the Bible says – ... *be fully convinced in his own mind* (Romans 14:5) about the subject.

For many years now when I have got up in the morning, I have said two things. The first is, 'Thank you Lord for the gift of life.' Remember that is a great privilege to be alive, and it is an aspect of God's mercy. Please thank Him for it when you get up. The second thing I say is, 'Perhaps you will come today Lord.' When we lived in Matlock in Derbyshire I used to go for a prayer walk in a nearby cemetery, and I loved to stand by the gravestone of a dear friend. On it was this simple inscription, 'Only till He come'. My prayer was 'O Lord, do you feel like coming now? I would love to be here to see the glorious commotion when the dead in Christ rise to meet you.' I am not a date fixer for too many people have made mistakes about the timing of His Coming, but I believe that having this attitude and expectation is a healthy way to live the Christian life. I wrote in chapter 3 –'The Christian's Hope' about the part that is our hope of His Coming. So, let us look into it. We start with a fact –

Jesus will come again

There are many witnesses to this fact.

Job said so hundreds of years before Jesus came for the first time – *I know that my Redeemer lives, and that in the end **he will stand upon the earth*** (Job 19:25).

Zechariah said so many years before Jesus came – *On that day **his feet will stand** on the Mount of Olives, east of Jerusalem, and the Mount of Olives will be split in two from east to west, forming a great valley, with half of the mountain moving north and half moving south* (Zechariah 14:4). So there will even be geographic proof of it!

Angels said so just after Jesus returned to heaven – *'Men of Galilee,' they said, 'why do you stand here looking into the sky? This same Jesus, who has been taken from you into heaven, **will come back** in the same way you have seen him go into heaven'* (Acts 1:11).

Jesus Himself said so – *At that time the sign of the Son of Man will appear in the sky, and all the nations of the earth will mourn. They will see **the Son of Man coming** on the clouds of the sky, with power and great glory* (Matthew 24:30). So there will be proof in the heavens of it.

God never tells lies

God is not a man, that he should lie, nor a son of man, that he should change his mind. Does he speak and then not act? Does he promise and not fulfil? (Numbers 23:19). If there is one thing which we can depend on, it is the fact that God means exactly what He says. In the world, diplomatic language is used; ambiguous terms which can be translated in many different ways are the order of the day. Even in churches people don't always say what they really mean. But we can rely on this fact about God – His Word is true. Even when our circumstances seem to say otherwise. God also made sure that His prophets told the truth when they wrote the Scriptures – *For prophecy never had its origin in the will of man, but men spoke from God as they were **carried along by the Holy Spirit*** (2 Peter 1:21).

No one can prevent Jesus coming

God challenges anyone to prevent Him from doing what He decides to do: *For the LORD Almighty has purposed, and who can thwart him? His hand is stretched out, and who can turn it back?* (Isaiah 14:27); *Yes, and from ancient days I am he. No one can deliver out of my hand. When I act, who can reverse it?* (Isaiah 43:13). Men can't prevent Him; the devil cannot prevent Him. The devil is very powerful, and he would love to prevent Jesus from coming again. But he cannot. Remember that the devil is not all powerful, because he is only a created being.

At Calvary the devil raised up his entire army to destroy Jesus. If he had succeeded, then Jesus would not be coming again. But Satan failed, utterly and completely. He was vanquished himself, how then can he prevent the Second Coming? J.B. Phillips translates Colossians 2:15 graphically – *and then, having drawn the sting of all the powers ranged against us, He exposed them, shattered, empty and defeated, in His final glorious act!* So, neither the devil nor men will stand in the way when God gives His Son the signal to come again.

Christians look forward to His Coming

His Coming is the prelude to Heaven. His Coming ushers in the events leading to the new Heaven and Earth; the time when all Creation is restored to the condition which God had in mind for it in the beginning. His Coming ushers us into His presence, to be where we have always wanted to be. We look forward to the Coming of Jesus because, like Abraham we are citizens of Heaven not earth – *By faith he made his home in the promised land **like a stranger in a foreign country**; he lived in tents, as did Isaac and Jacob, who were heirs with him of the same promise* (Hebrews 11:9). We have no abiding home here – *For here we do not have an enduring city, but we are looking for the city that is to come*

(Hebrews 13:14). When Jesus returns He will lead us into that City. What a city! What a God!

Most Christians long for His Coming, like those described in the Bible who – *longed for his appearing* (2 Timothy 4:8). This is especially true in places such as China where life for Christians is grim indeed. All through the centuries Christians have been persecuted and have looked and longed for Jesus to come again. The disciples were slow at first to believe Him when He promised to return, but eventually they began to look forward to His Coming, but only when our thoughtful Saviour sent an angel to help them. The angel came to the discouraged group of disciples and said – *Men of Galilee, . . . why do you stand here looking into the sky? This same Jesus, who has been taken from you into heaven, will come back in the same way you have seen him go into heaven* (Acts 1:11). At first, all they could think of was the loss of their Master, and that they would not survive the loss of Him. In addition they might well have thought that they would not be able to minister without Him. But, comforted by angelic assurance, they pressed on with the work, and looked forward to His coming again – as we should.

Therefore, 'exhort one another every day'

Seeing that we are looking for His coming, we might as well remind one another of the fact constantly. It helps to keep our hope alive. God listens to see if we do talk about His Coming and Heaven. Exhortation is something of a lost art. Let us reinstate it. To exhort one another means to encourage, to urge on, to entreat each other. It is scriptural – *But encourage* (exhort) *one another daily, as long as it is called Today* (Hebrews 3:13). Our meetings give us the best chance to exhort each other. As long as we are obeying the Scripture – *Let us not give up meeting together, as some are in the habit of doing, but let us encourage one another – and all the more **as you see the Day approaching*** (Hebrews 10:25). Let us do so while we can. Remember what James said about the imminence of the Lord's coming – . . . *The*

*Judge is standing **at the door!*** (James 5:9). Here is a good way to start exhorting each other. Use this word ***Maranatha*** (1 Corinthians 16:22). It can be translated either as 'Our Lord **will** come', or as 'Come, O Lord!' Either way, it is a good exhortation. Let us use it instead of the standard greeting – 'Hallo, how are you?' 'Fine thanks, how are you?' 'Fine thanks' may be true or it may not be true. The church contains some evangelical liars! Perhaps a good response to 'Maranatha' should be the words in Scripture – . . . *Amen. Come, Lord Jesus* (Revelation 22:20).

The whole world will see His Coming

We are used to the world's events coming into our homes via the TV. Mostly we see bad news, but on the day that is in God's diary, something will happen which will be good news to the Christian, and bad news for the anti-Christian.

Jesus will come. He will come in the sight of every living being. I once thought that everyone would need to have a TV in order that *every eye should see Him.* But of course the Bible does not say that Jesus will come in the twinkling of an eye, but that we would be **changed** in the twinkling of an eye. *Listen, I tell you a mystery: We will not all sleep, but we will all be **changed** – in a flash, in the twinkling of an eye, at the last trumpet. For the trumpet will sound, the dead will be raised imperishable, and we will be changed* (1 Corinthians 15:51–52). So, Jesus could show Himself by means of the TV, or He could stand in the heavens for 24 hours while the globe rotated if He wishes so that every eye should see Him. Or He could work a miracle of revelation. The method does not matter; the fact is that He is coming – **visibly**. This fact is emphasised by Scripture – *On that day his feet will stand on the Mount of Olives, east of Jerusalem, and the Mount of Olives will be split in two from east to west, forming a great valley, with half of the mountain moving north and half moving south* (Zechariah 14:4). I cannot see how this Scripture can be fulfilled without any one noticing it! It will be the most public event in history.

This will be no secret Rapture. The following are some of the noisiest verses in the Bible – *For the Lord himself will come down from Heaven, with a loud command, with the voice of **the archangel** and with the trumpet call of God, and the dead in Christ will rise first. After that, we who are still alive and are left will be caught up together with them in the clouds to meet the Lord in the air. And so we will be **with the Lord** for ever. Therefore encourage each other with these words* (1 Thessalonians 4:16–18).

Reasons for His Coming

To gather His people

Just think how dear we are to Jesus. He has such a passionate love for us, therefore he passionately desires to have us with Him in Heaven. Try and sense His deep longing in this Scripture – *Father, I want those you have given me to be with me where I am, and to see my glory, the glory you have given me because you loved me before the creation of the world* (John 17:24). One great reason for the Second Coming is for God to sweep us up into His arms and take us to be with Him forever. How we will glorify Him and marvel at Him – *on the day he comes to be glorified in his holy people and to be marvelled at among all those who have believed. This includes you, because you believed our testimony to you* (2 Thessalonians 1:10).

I often see a lovely vision of Jesus coming for His Bride, the church. In it I seem to see great activity in Heaven. Angels are making preparation for some great event, such as the crowning of a King. They are excited and, while they are making preparations, they still keep an eye on the Lord Jesus. He is sitting on the Throne and He keeps looking at His Father with a lovely expression, perhaps with a question in His heart. Eventually the Father says to Him 'go now and bring your Bride into Glory'. Immediately huge crowds of angels form a corridor from heaven to the cloudy heavens. God the Holy Spirit takes some senior angels and comes to the earth with them. They single out all the true people of God, ignoring many who go to church but are not born again. From every nation and denomination the Spirit calls out those who are God's people. It seems as if he has a smile on His face as He introduces the Brethren to the converted Catholics, and the Anglicans to the Pentecostals! There are millions of us, and yet, as we begin to move up into the heavens through this vast corridor of angels, we all seem to merge into one person. Meanwhile Jesus has been coming down that same corridor to meet us.

Millions of heavenly beings are assembled to watch the spectacle. There are roars of approval as Jesus steps forward to receive us, His Bride. Everything in Creation shouting aloud with joy and wonder. And our voices join in with praise and exhilaration as we are joined forever to the One we love. The Spirit then joins us to Jesus and He leads us in great dignity and majesty into Heaven. The angels are craning their necks as they exclaim to one another 'this is the Bride of the Saviour, how glorious she is'. (Perhaps it is this time that the Scripture depicts) – *Then I heard what sounded like a great multitude, like the roar of rushing waters and like loud peals of thunder, shouting: 'Hallelujah! For our Lord God Almighty reigns. Let us rejoice and be glad and give him glory! For the wedding of the Lamb has come, and his bride has made herself ready. Fine linen, bright and clean, was given her to wear.' (Fine linen stands for the righteous acts of the saints.)* (Revelation 19:6–8). Jesus then leads us to the Throne and probably says 'Father, here is my Bride', and the Father welcomes us saying 'welcome to the realm of everlasting Day, where unity is normal and grief is unknown. Come to your Home prepared before the world was made'. Then Jesus ascends a Throne, and in some way we become individuals again as we kneel before Him. He then causes an angel to read out the record of our lives, rewarding everything we have done that was worthy of reward. (There follows an amazing time of worship and exhilaration). After this we become as one person again as Jesus leads us into a wonderful banqueting Hall. Here we are served and attended by angels as we sit closely next to Jesus and He shares many of the secrets of eternity with us. The scene changes again as we are led through a vast arch into a rather mysterious realm. I get the impression of great kingdoms, and vast areas of beautiful territory. But then, to my great disappointment, the vision fades, and I am left in tears of joy mingled with frustration because the vision fades.

To resurrect the dead

I have dealt with this in chapter 20 – 'The Judgement Day' as far as the unsaved dead are concerned, and in chapter 8 – 'There will be a Resurrection' as far as the saved are concerned.

To judge the world. To bring justice

*In faithfulness he will **bring forth justice*** (Isaiah 42:3). Jesus will come – *to judge everyone, and to convict all the ungodly of all the ungodly acts they have done in the ungodly way, and of all the harsh words ungodly sinners have spoken against him* (Jude 1:15).

I have dealt with this in chapter 20 – 'The Judgement Day'.

To renew Creation

The beautiful world which God created was spoiled by the entry of sin. In the beginning God saw His Creation and pronounced it to be good. There were no weeds, nothing destructive, and no pollution.

The animals ate herbs, and were not 'red in tooth and claw'. There were no wars, famines, or disease. This is how He wanted it to be. But after Satan poisoned the hearts of man and woman, the world began to be spoiled. Fear, murder, greed, jealousy, and rebellion began to change the earth into a dark and sad place. Basically it is still the same today although it is not all doom and gloom. Jesus is building His church, and the devil's darkness has not extinguished the light of God. But, there is hope of a better world because Jesus is coming again, and He will change it.

All Creation looks for His Coming – *The creation waits in eager expectation for the sons of God to be revealed ... that the creation itself will be liberated from its bondage to decay and brought into the glorious freedom of the children of God* (Romans 8:19 & 21).

More about this in chapter 14 – 'The Kingdom'.

To enforce the triumph of Calvary

Jesus destroyed the power of the devil and all his works at Calvary, as the Bible says – *The reason the Son of God appeared was to destroy the devil's work* (1 John 3:8), but the trouble is that Satan has managed to delude people into thinking that he is still in charge of this world. He reckons to be lord of the world, therefore Jesus will come and show that there is only one Lord as the Bible declares – *and every tongue confess that **Jesus Christ is Lord**, to the glory of God the Father* (Philippians 2:11). What a thrilling proof of His Lordship we have in this verse – *And then the lawless one will be revealed, whom the Lord Jesus will overthrow with the **breath of his mouth** and destroy by the splendor of his coming* (2 Thessalonians 2:8). What a world it will be when Jesus reigns in total visible power, and is publicly vindicated in the sight of all Creation. My prayer is 'Come dear Lord – as soon as possible.'

No one knows when Jesus will come again

*No one knows about that day or hour, not even the angels in heaven, **nor the Son**, but only the Father* (Matthew 24:36). In the light of this dogmatic statement by God, we would think that nobody would be silly enough to fix dates, yet there are several groups who think that they have special revelation about the Second Coming. People such as the so-called Jehovah Witnesses, despite the fact that they have come unstuck time after time with their ridiculous date-fixing. If Jesus does not know the date, how can any mortal man? No one knows the date, but we must be ready – on the alert for our Lord's arrival. He gives no promise of a warning in advance, only general indications – *But the day of the Lord will come like a thief . . .* (2 Peter 3:10). Let us make sure that we are alert for this wonderful event, because from God's point of view, His Coming is always 'near'. We have to remember that God does not live in the same time/space dimension as we do. We only have 24 hours in a day, whereas . . . *With the Lord a day is like a **thousand years**, and a **thousand years** are like a day* (2 Peter 3:8). I have to confess that I sometimes say to God 'O Lord, I believe this Scripture, but with me a thousand years is a very very long time.' The years go by and some prayers are not answered. How vital it is to have an eternal perspective! God's environment is eternal. Time is irrelevant there. It is always 'today'.

Therefore live in the light of His coming

Use the gift of time as well as we can

While we are alive, we have opportunities. We can either use them, or lose them. That is why God urges us to use them while the going is good – *making the most of every **opportunity**, because the days are evil* (Ephesians 5:16). How much time do we have left? No one knows for sure, and we cannot even be sure that we will be alive tomorrow. That is why James 4:13–17 warns us against boasting about tomorrow . . . *for you do not know what a day may bring forth* (Proverbs 27:1). While we have time we can use it in a number of ways. We can –

Work as Jesus did

He came to work for His Father – *Then he said, 'Here I am, I have come to do your will.' He sets aside the first to establish the second* (Hebrews 10:9). He also had a divine compulsion within His heart which caused Him to say – *As long as it is day, **we must** do the work of him who sent me. **Night is coming**, when no one can work* (John 9:4). He was never frantic about it, but He did not waste His time and opportunities. If we love Him, neither will we waste ours.

We can –
– Work by winning more souls. Evangelising with real urgency and zeal.
– Work by preparing the way for Revival. *Prepare the way for the Lord, make straight paths for him* (Mark 1:3).
– Work by praying for the nation and the area in which God has put us.
– Lay up more treasure in Heaven.
– Become more holy or sanctified (more like Jesus).

By doing these things we will speed His coming – *as you look forward to the day of God and speed its coming* (2 Peter 3:12), and I cannot think of a better way of doing so than to win souls, as well as the other activities. Let us do it!

Be ready to give an account

How gracious God is to give us advanced warning of Jesus' Coming, and the fact that accounts will be required – *So then, each of us will give an account of himself to God* (Romans 14:12). We need not be worried at this prospect, unless we are deliberately hanging on to sin in our lives. God will remember every **good** thing we have done and He will enjoy reading those things out! Just make sure that we have a healthy fear, and make sure that it is a **healthy** fear, not an unreasoning terror. Aim to see Him when He comes without the need to blush. You could be ashamed or embarrassed if you are slow to witness for example, so make sure that you are not ashamed to speak about Him to the world outside. He Has said – *If anyone is ashamed of me and my words in this adulterous and sinful generation, the Son of Man will be ashamed of him when he comes in his Father's glory with the holy angels* (Mark 8:38). God is not sentimental, He speaks quite bluntly when He warns us that – *whoever disowns me before men, I will disown him before my Father in heaven* (Matthew 10:33). Take the Apostle John's fatherly advice – *And now, dear children, continue in him, so that when he appears we may be confident and unashamed before him at his coming* (1 John 2:28).

I have written more about this in chapter 11 – 'The Judgement Seat of Christ'.

Living this way is practical

It encourages us to be spiritually healthy.

It stimulates evangelism, prayer, holiness, and heavenly mindedness.

Living this way is possible

God Himself will help us – *So do not fear, for I am with you; do not be dismayed, for I am your God. I will strengthen you and help you; I will uphold you with my righteous right hand* (Isaiah 41:10).

And I will ask the Father, and he will give you another Counsellor to be with you forever (John 14:16).

My prayer for all of us is – *May he strengthen your hearts so that you will be blameless and holy in the presence of our God and Father when our Lord Jesus comes with all his holy ones* (1 Thessalonians 3:13).

Our Lord will come – will He find us ready? Make sure now.

I close this chapter with a verse of a hymn by H.G. Spafford which expresses the Christian's deep longings –

> But Lord, 'tis for Thee, for Thy Coming we wait,
> The sky, not the grave, is our goal:
> Oh, trump of the angel! oh voice of the Lord!
> Blessed hope! blessed rest of my soul.

What a joy to be able to sing the chorus to the hymn – 'It is well, it is well with my soul'.

Not only will Jesus come again to judge the world – banish Satan – resurrect the dead and all the other things, but His Coming will be the prelude to His Wedding! More about it in the next chapter.

Chapter 10

The Wedding of Christ

One day there will be a stirring in Heaven. Its occupants will be getting ready for a great occasion. Is it a Coronation? Partly, but it is also a Wedding. The occasion when Jesus and His Bride are joined together forever. Scripture describes it – *Let us rejoice and be glad and give him glory! For the wedding of the Lamb has come, and his bride has made herself ready* (Revelation 19:7). The 'Lamb' in this verse is Jesus. John identifies Him for us in his Gospel – *When he saw Jesus passing by, he said, 'Look, the **Lamb of God!'** * (John 1:36). The 'Bridegroom' in Revelation 19:7 is Jesus. The context in John's Gospel makes it plain that Jesus is speaking about Himself as the Bridegroom. *Jesus answered, 'How can the guests of the bridegroom fast while he is with them? They cannot, so long as they have him with them'* (Mark 2:19). Many men remember as I do, the day of their wedding. What excitement, what anticipation we experienced. Amazingly enough, Jesus is excited at the prospect of His great Day too. Just think how precious you are to Him! There is an Old Testament parallel to this wedding – God called the nation of Israel His wife – *For your Maker is your husband – the Lord Almighty is his name* (Isaiah 54:5). God loved Israel dearly as a man loves his wife, and He was committed to her forever. He said so in those lovely words in Scripture – *I will betroth you to me for ever...* (Hosea 2:19). Jesus says a similar thing to His

Bride, the Church – *Never will I leave you; never will I forsake you* (Hebrews 13:5).

The Bride is the true church

John the Apostle was given a preview of this Wedding, when an angel said to him – ... *Come, I will show you the bride, the wife of the Lamb* (Revelation 21:9). Because God wants us to have something of a preview, He commanded John to record it for us, so that we could get excited and prepared for it. *Then the angel said to me, 'Write: "Blessed are those who are invited to the wedding supper of the Lamb".'* (Revelation 19:9). When we were born again, we were invited by Jesus to come to Him that we may have life – ... *I have come that they may have life, and have it to the full* (John 10:10). When we came and received that life, we became His people. One description of us – His people – was that of His Bride. Now we are no longer our own, we have a new Head – *For the husband is the head of the wife as Christ is the head of the church, his body, of which he is the Saviour* (Ephesians 5:23). As Jesus rightly said – *The bride belongs to the bridegroom...* (John 3:29). In the words of a lovely hymn by G. Wade Robinson – 'Loved with everlasting love ... His forever, **only** His; who the Lord and me shall part...?

Jesus is jealous over His Bride

Again I quote *The bride belongs to the bridegroom...* (John 3:29). If she belongs to anyone else, she is adulterous. Anyone who is truly in love will feel a jealousy and a legitimate possessiveness towards his beloved. Jesus' love is jealous too, although there is no malice in His jealousy. The Bible illustrates this – *Do not worship any other god, for the LORD, whose name is Jealous, is a jealous God* (Exodus 34:14). His love for us is deep and sacrificial – ... *Christ loved the church and gave himself up for her* (Ephesians 5:25). In return He looks for similar devotion. It is both our duty and our privilege to surrender our lives completely to Him. Surrender is one of the best proofs that we are truly born again.

Her garments

What bride would arrive on her wedding day in a filthy coat, muddy gumboots, matted hair, and an unwashed face! To do so would be an insult to her husband, and an embarrassment to all the guests. So, on the great Wedding Day of the Son of God, He will expect to find us, His Bride, clean, beautified, and radiant. Will He find you like that? View the scene again from Scripture – ... *For the wedding of the Lamb has come, and his bride has **made herself ready*** (Revelation 19:7). We must make ourselves ready, and He gives us all the help we need to do so. Think what He has done in order *to make her holy, cleansing her by the washing with water through the word, and to present her to himself as a radiant church, without stain or wrinkle or any other blemish, but holy and blameless* (Ephesians 5:26, 27). He has made it possible for us to be beautiful, now let us make use of the Divine facilities in order to be ready and desirable for Him.

The Bride's garments are not earthly ones; they would not impress Heaven's angels. In lovely pictorial language the Bible describes the things which make us beautiful in the sight of God – *'Fine linen, bright and clean, was given her to wear.' (**Fine linen stands for the righteous acts of the saints.**)* (Revelation 19:8). 'Righteous acts' are the evidence on earth of a godly holy life. But before we could 'wear' such 'garments' we needed to become capable of doing so. God enabled us by clothing us with salvation. In other words He gave us the kind of life which transformed us from the ugliness of sin into the beauty of holiness – ... *my God. For he has clothed me with **garments of salvation** and arrayed me in a **robe of righteousness**, as a bridegroom adorns his head like a priest, and as a bride adorns herself with her jewels* (Isaiah 61:10). No wonder that our beloved

Lord can now look at us so beautifully clothed and say – *All beautiful you are, my darling; there is no flaw in you* (Song of Songs 4:7). You might say 'no flaw' Lord? I can find plenty in this heart of mine. If you do, He may well reply, saying 'I know all your weaknesses, and of course I will deal with them, but for the moment please hear Me say that I see My righteousness in you, and the work of My Spirit in you as He continues to conform you into My Image. That is why I say there is no flaw in you.' Let us remember that Jesus, the Bridegroom, is deeply in love with us, His Bride. Our enemy loves to deny this, and he is delighted when we doubt His love, as most Christians do.

God the Holy Spirit is steadily making us more and more like Jesus, provided that we co-operate with Him. But again, the devil and our own tendency to denigrate ourselves conspire to make us doubt that we are becoming more Christlike. But why not give the Holy Sprit the credit for what He **is** doing in us, and why not take the encouragement of being at least somewhat Christlike? Listen to the Bridegroom, and let Him thrill you and enjoy you – *You have stolen my heart, my sister, my bride; you have stolen my heart with one glance of your eyes, with one jewel of your necklace* (Song of Songs 4:9). If you have won the heart of God the Son, you must be special!

You need the right garments for this Wedding. Anyone found without the garment of Salvation will be cast out immediately. Heaven has no place for those who reckon that their garment of good works will suffice for Heaven. The Bible warns about this error – *'Friend,' he asked, 'how did you get in here without wedding clothes?' The man was speechless* (Matthew 22:12).

Let no one fool around with God. If you want to be at this wedding, don't play around. Let nothing get in the way of your preparation for it. Don't make excuses. Hear the Word of God again – *Jesus replied: 'A certain man was preparing a great banquet and invited many guests. At the time of the banquet he sent his servant to tell those who had been invited, "Come, for everything is now ready." But they all alike began to make excuses. The first said, "I have just bought a field, and I must go and see it. Please excuse me."'* (Luke 14:16–18). Attendance at this Wedding must be a priority – can you really resist an invitation like the one in the Bible – *The Spirit and the bride say, 'Come!'* (Revelation 22:17). What is your answer going to be? Are you going to respond?

Another thing about this wedding is that the Bride must be pure. Jesus wants a virgin Bride. He is thinking of spiritual purity of course. Those who are saved but who were immoral are not disqualified as long as they have repented and turned away from immoral behaviour. Remember Mary Magdalen? How lovely it is when a couple come to their wedding day as virgins. Virginity is rather unpopular today, but at least there are some who observe it. How lovely it is when Christians preserve their spiritual purity, and by doing so get ready to greet Jesus with joy. Paul had this in mind when he said that he longed to present the Christians to Jesus as a pure Bride. He said – *'I am jealous for you with a godly jealousy. I promised you to one husband, to Christ, so that I might present you as a pure virgin to him'* (2 Corinthians 11:2). If you are not pure in your spiritual life or your sexual life at the moment, then come to Him confessing your sin of immorality whether that be spiritual or physical, and ask for His forgiveness. He will grant it to you and then you will be ready for the Wedding. How exciting!.

The wedding supper is a celebration

This Wedding Supper is open to all who will be His Bride. Are you a Christian? Are you His Bride? You can be, if you want to be. And if you are ready for total surrender to God. Then you can celebrate and take the great Communion. I believe that this Wedding includes the Communion which Jesus mentioned when He said – *'For I tell you, I will not eat it* (the Passover/Communion) *again until it finds fulfilment in the kingdom of God'* (Luke 22:16). I believe it will take place in that wonderful Banqueting Hall in Heaven. We can only guess at the form it will take, but it will be wonderful when Jesus takes part in it with us.

The wedding is delayed

At the moment Jesus (the Bridegroom) and the Church (the Bride) are only **betrothed**, not **married**. The stage is being set in Heaven, the final preparations are probably in hand; it only awaits the signal from God the Father for Jesus to come, and then, we shall be joined – forever. Meanwhile let us get ready for this great Day in which we will . . . *rejoice and be glad and give him glory!* (Revelation 19:7). Then, as if Jesus' Coming and the Wedding is not exciting enough, there is another thing in store for us in Heaven. It is the Judgement Seat of Christ – the time for accounts and rewards. Read about it in the next chapter.

Chapter 11

The Judgement Seat of Christ

I am not sure about the sequence of the great events which we are considering in this book. There are many theories, charts and books about the sequence, but I do not feel that it is important enough to spend a great deal of time considering them. The Bible simply states some things and does not go into minute detail. The biblical fact that we are considering here is that there will be an event called 'The Judgement Seat' or 'Throne', which is mentioned in Scripture – *For we must all appear before the judgment seat of Christ...* (2 Corinthians 5:10). This Throne is almost certainly the same Judgement Seat or Throne as that in Revelation 20:11 – *Then I saw a great white throne and him who was seated on it* (Revelation 20:11). I believe that there is only one Throne of God, but different aspects of it. Although Jesus will judge the whole world, I am only dealing in this chapter with His judgement or assessment of Christians. (I write about the rest in chapter 20 – 'The Judgement Day'.) It will be at this Throne that this Judge will give Christians their rewards.

There is only one Judge on it

The Judge is Jesus. As the Bible says – *Moreover, the Father judges no one, but has entrusted all judgement to the Son* (John 5:22). Jesus is described in the Bible as the Son –

When the Son of Man comes in his glory, and all the angels with him, he will sit on his throne in heavenly glory (Matthew 25:31). Jesus as the Judge will determine, on the basis of all the evidence, what is right for the saved. He will give rewards to some of His people, which may be large or small, but others may have no rewards. When Jesus has completed His public assessment of us He will announce His verdict – *Then the King will say to those on his right, 'Come, you who are blessed by my Father; take your inheritance, the kingdom prepared for you since the creation of the world'* (Matthew 25:34). Elsewhere in Scripture he says, *For the Son of Man is going to come in his Father's glory with his angels, and then he will reward each person according to what he has done* (Matthew 16:27).

This judgement will be a very thorough assessment of what we have done, thought and said during our lifetime. Every one of our words, thoughts, and actions has been recorded. God has missed nothing, and all will be revealed. *This will take place on the day when God will judge men's secrets through Jesus Christ, as my gospel declares* (Romans 2:16). *But I tell you that men will have to give account on the day of judgement for every careless word they have spoken* (Matthew 12:36). How wonderful it is, in the light of this, that we can trust in the fact that God has forgiven all confessed sins, and has blotted them out of the record. These things will **not** be read out in the great Day! But those lovely things which Christians say to one another about God **will** be read out. *Then those who feared the* LORD *talked with each other, and the* LORD *listened and heard. A scroll of remembrance was written in his presence concerning those who feared the* LORD *and honoured his name* (Malachi 3:16).

Having said that, there is still a possibility of being ashamed at this Judgement Seat, because we may neglect to keep our hearts clean, or to become apathetic in our walk with God. If Jesus comes, and we are still harbouring sin in our lives, then the record stands, and it will be read out on that Day. If this brings fear to us, it is probably healthy fear! Let the Scripture warn us – *And now, dear children, continue in him, so that when he appears we may be confident and unashamed before him at his coming* (1 John 2:28). So it is possible for us to avoid shame, but only if we are careful. It is not easy to confess our sin before our fellow Christians, but it is better to be embarrassed down here rather than up There. Jesus is so merciful, and so ready to forgive. He is utterly straight with us, but will always be gracious. Consider what the Bible says about Him – ... *the One and Only, who came from the Father,* **full of grace and truth** (John 1:14). If we are afraid that we have gone too far, and hesitate to draw near to this Holy One, look at the Scripture – *Let us then approach the throne of grace with confidence, so that we may receive mercy and find grace to help us in our time of need* (Hebrews 4:16). See His face, glowing with love for us, only too willing to respond to repentance with His mercy; why wait?

Rewards are given at this Judgement Seat

Few Christians believe that God will reward them in Heaven. They believe that God will reward the great people such as Paul, but not the more ordinary people. If someone tells them that God has rewards waiting for them in Heaven, they usually react in disbelief, and speak of the dangers of getting proud. But there is a danger of mock modesty too! Let us get rid of it.

Why do we brush aside the promise of rewards?

False humility is just as bad as pride. In fact it is inverted pride. The fear of pride, or the danger of seeming to be proud is one of the main reasons why Christians brush this matter of rewards aside. And yet it is an insult to the Lord Jesus to do so! Every sincere Christian will desire to honour the Lord on the earth; that is why we labour hard for Him in our work. Similarly, every sincere Christian needs the encouragement of knowing that they are doing well, and that God is noticing their work. He does, according to Scripture – *God is not unjust; he will not forget your work and the love you have shown him as you have helped his people and continue to help them* (Hebrews 6:10). Why then do we shrink from the idea of receiving our rewards in Heaven? It has nothing to do with pride; it has everything to do with honouring God.

Jesus exhorts us to seek for rewards

Do not store up for yourselves treasures on earth, where moth and rust destroy, and where thieves break in and steal. But store up for yourselves treasures in heaven, where moth and rust do not destroy, and where thieves do not break in and steal (Matthew 6:19–20). As long as our motives are pure we can respond to His injunction. If we aim for rewards in order to show off, then we are in real danger. God said so – ... *God* **opposes the proud** *but gives grace to the humble* (1 Peter 5:5). But if we aim for rewards in loving response to what He plainly commands us, how can we go wrong? Let us get rid of this sinful mock modesty, and trust our firm and loving Father to keep us from pride.

God gives wages to His labourers

He laid down the principle of a fair day's work for a fair day's pay. He is honourable to His own workers, and He expects human employers to honour their workers. *For the Scripture says, 'Do not muzzle the ox while it is treading out the grain,' and 'The worker deserves his wages'* (1 Timothy 5:18). A Christian employer who is miserly in the wages he gives will not find the approval of God. Nor will those miserly church leaders who give a pittance to those who come and minister to his people. A dear friend of mine who has a travelling ministry (one of the finest I know), sometimes says to the Treasurer of the church 'I don't want a lovegift, I want my wages.' I applaud him, because he is scriptural in what he says – *For the Scripture says, ... 'The worker deserves **his wages'** (1 Timothy 5:18).

God gives rewards to His servants

As well as giving wages, God gives rewards to His servants. That is if they are overcomers, for the Bible only mentions rewards to those who overcome their lusts and difficulties. But if God finds overcomers, He responds to them and rewards them even though He does not need to do so. For example, God says, ***To him who overcomes**, I will give the right to sit with me on my throne, just as I overcame and sat down with my Father on his throne* (Revelation 3:21). This word 'overcomers' is repeated all through Revelation chapters 2–3. So rewards are not given lightly, and only to those who prove faithful on earth. Perhaps I should utter a further warning here. It is possible to lose rewards, because we are all likely to fail if we are not very careful. God warns us of the possibility – *Watch out that you do not lose what you have worked for, but that you may be rewarded fully* (2 John 1:8). And again – *If what he has built **survives**, he will receive his reward* (1 Corinthians 3:14). It would be such a pity if we failed after doing so well at first. But we don't need to fail, because God offers us all the help we need to keep going.

Rewards are over and above wages. They are not deserved, but they are given as a sovereign act of a Sovereign God, as He chooses. Nevertheless, if some of His people are more faithful than others, He surely takes note of it. For example, Paul and others like him will be rewarded to a far greater extent than I will, because he was more faithful, sacrificial, and fruitful than I am. It is still true that Paul does not deserve anything, but he received assurance from God that he would have a crown – *Now there is in store for me the **crown of righteousness**, which the Lord, the righteous Judge, will award to me on that day – and not only to me, but also to all who have longed for his appearing* (2 Timothy 4:8). God grant that I may be among them, and you too!

This all leaves a bit of a problem because the Bible says – *So you also, when you have done everything you were told to do, should say, 'We are unworthy servants; we have only done our duty'* (Luke 17:10). And yet Scripture also mentions rewards, even for small things such as a drink – *I tell you the truth, anyone who gives you a cup of water in my name because you belong to Christ will certainly not lose his reward* (Mark 9:41). How generous God is. He goes on the speak about other rewards – *'I tell you the truth,' Jesus replied, 'no one who has left home or brothers or sisters or mother or father or children or fields for me and the gospel will fail to receive a hundred times as much in this present age (homes, brothers, sisters, mothers, children and fields – and with them, persecutions) and in the age to come, eternal life'* (Mark 10:29–30). My own conclusion is that I am a servant, and I deserve nothing but my wages. But, knowing the greatheartedness of God, and accepting His Word about rewards, I will aim for them, believing that my reception of them in Glory will glorify the name of Jesus. The main thing in this verse in Luke is that we should not get proud of what we do for God, and we must certainly avoid taking the credit for what God chooses to do through us.

What are the rewards?

Scripture does not give many details, but there are a few clues.

There are places of honour – *but to sit at my right or left is not for me to grant. These places belong to those for whom they have been prepared* (Mark 10:40).

There are kingdoms, or at least spheres of authority – *if we endure, we will also **reign** with him* (2 Timothy 2:12). How can we reign without a kingdom?

There are crowns which are usually the symbol of kingship – *Now there is in store for me the crown of righteousness, which the Lord, the righteous Judge, will award to me on that day – and not only to me, but also to all who have longed for his appearing* (2 Timothy 4:8).

There are positions in the stewardship of Creation – *His master replied, 'Well done, good and faithful servant! You have been faithful with a few things; I will put you in charge of many things. Come and share your master's happiness!'* (Matthew 25:23). More about this point in chapter 14 – 'The Kingdom'.

The details may be scarce, but the fact of rewards is plain in Scripture. Therefore we must not let false modesty prevent us from pressing towards them.

Rewards are not our major aim

Although it is right for us to look for rewards in Heaven, our primary aim is to work in a way that pleases God. As Paul said – *So we make it our goal to **please him**, whether we are at home in the body or away from it* (2 Corinthians 5:9). Paul gives us another healthy worthwhile objective – *Whatever you do, work at it with all your heart, as **working for the Lord**, not for men* (Colossians 3:23), but please notice that in the next verse he mentions our rewards as well as our work – *since you know that you will receive an inheritance from the Lord as a reward. It is the Lord Christ you are serving* (Colossians 3:24). It pleases God when He sees us standing before Him in Heaven with plenty to show for our labours on the earth.

Our triumphal entry to Heaven

My own expectation when I enter Heaven is to hear a fanfare from angels announcing my arrival in Heaven. Not because I reckon to be famous, but simply because of the value which God sets on us as individuals. I hope then to see a pile of rewards with my name on them. Then, it will be a tremendous joy to take them one by one and to kneel before the Lord Jesus, saying 'Lord, you gave these rewards to me because of my service on earth; it is now my great joy to give them back to you as an act of worship.' I hope to repeat this until the pile is finished. It will be a bit like the elders in

Heaven of whom it is written – *They lay their crowns before the throne.* By the way, the attention of Heaven's occupants will not be centred upon me, it will be upon the Lord Jesus. They will not be saying 'O Lord, how wonderful is Alexander Buchanan' – not at all – rather will they be saying 'How wonderful you are O God, how you have glorified yourself through this son of yours.' My point is this – if I have no rewards up there, I am less able to glorify Jesus. The greater the pile, the more glory I bring to the Lord Jesus. It has nothing to do with pride, but it has everything to do with worship. Work then, in a way in which God can reward us, and let's be quick about it – *Behold, I am coming soon! My reward is with me, and I will give to everyone according to what he has done* (Revelation 22:12).

Look forward to this Throne, and these rewards

Having written about our joy and rewards in Heaven, let me urge us to rejoice here and now in the expectation of being at this Throne of God – *But rejoice that you participate in the sufferings of Christ, so that you may be **overjoyed** when his glory is revealed* (1 Peter 4:13). And again – *Therefore you ... **eagerly wait** for our Lord Jesus Christ to be revealed* (1 Corinthians 1:7). Looking forward to being rewarded is quite scriptural. Jesus reminds us again of the fact of rewards – *Behold, I am coming soon! My reward is with me, and I will give to everyone according to what he has done* (Revelation 22:12).

But what happens after we have joyfully received our rewards and our assignments from God? We will be so exhilarated that we will need a prolonged time of worship. But what is worship? ...

Chapter 12

Worship in Heaven

Worship is one of Heaven's great occupations

Heaven is full of worship all the time. I used to wonder how we would sustain it throughout eternity. Surely there was a limit to the songs we could sing! But, if everyone who is born again is to give an adequate testimony, and because each one will lead to a fresh outburst of praise and worship, we will need eternity to do it! There must be millions and millions of Christians, and they will all be in Heaven. All will be eager to tell of God's goodness – so, where is the problem?

Apart from all this, we will be in creative mood all the time, so there will surely be a constant flow of new songs, praises etc. We will have new bodies then, with new minds to go with them. We will be creative in our thinking, and inspired all the time there. We also have new tongues, and this will enable us all to sing beautifully and always in tune. David gave a little indication of our mood in Heaven – *Therefore my **heart is glad** and my **tongue rejoices**; my body also will rest secure* (Psalm 16:9). How can anyone remain silent when God is around? Scripture says *You have made known to me the path of life; you will fill me with **joy in your presence**, with eternal pleasures at your right hand* (Psalm 16:11). Heaven is not a dull place. God is not miserable, but vibrant, emotional, joyful – an inspiration to all around

Him. So we are likely to be quite excited there. Exuberance is a characteristic of worship in Heaven, and it is not wrong. It is not wrong to get some practice down here either. Truly worship will be a major occupation in Heaven. Not forgetting that worship includes service.

God loves real worship

He loves it, and looks for true worship. He finds it on earth through us, and He will find it through us even more in Heaven. We will be able to outdo the angels for we know about redemption. The angels will expect us to do so. We will be exhilarated by the prospect of exploring the Creation – hearing God's answers to our questions – making continual discoveries – and enjoying our new bodies. We shall undoubtedly worship God for such blessings. The atmosphere is captured in these wonderful verses – *Then I looked and heard the voice of many angels, numbering thousands upon thousands, and ten thousand times ten thousand. They encircled the throne and the living creatures and the elders* (Revelation 5:11). *All the angels were standing around the throne and around the elders and the four living creatures. They fell down on their faces before the throne and worshipped God* (Revelation 7:11). *And they sang a new song before the throne and before the four living creatures and the elders. No one could learn the song except the 144,000 who had been redeemed from the earth* (Revelation 14:3). By God's grace we are among them!

God will enjoy Himself in Heaven. He will enjoy having us there. He has anticipated it since we were born again, or perhaps since before the world was made! The Bible says – *Yet a time is coming and has now come when the true worshippers will worship the Father in spirit and truth, for they are the kind of worshippers the Father seeks. God is spirit, and his worshippers must worship in spirit and in truth* (John 4:23–24). One of the great privileges in Heaven will be to give Him what he loves, i.e. genuine worship. This verse in The Amplified Bible says ... *in truth and reality.*

Those who love God will make sure that they bring Him real worship on earth, so that they are well prepared to give it to Him in Heaven. Heaven's worship is pleasant to God. It is fragrant to Him. Paul says – *For we are to God the* **aroma** *of Christ among those who are being saved and those who are perishing* (2 Corinthians 2:15). We are a great joy to God as His people, and we give Him that which is fragrant to Him – our worship. What a privilege, what a responsibility!

A definition of worship

That which is drawn out of our hearts by the Holy Spirit as he shows God to us, either from the Bible, or through preaching, or by prophetic revelation. Service, and the attitude in which we serve God is an aspect of worship. Music and singing are an important but not necessarily the major aspect of worship. Worship is featured in the whole Bible, but because this book is primarily about Heaven, we will only look at worship in the Book of Revelation. Hopefully we will be able to see what God means by worship and then we may have to change our understanding of what we call worship. Several Greek words will help us to understand worship. I deal with them later in the chapter.

John's vision of Heaven's worship

It centred on God and His Son

And when he had taken it, the four living creatures and the twenty-four elders fell down before **the Lamb** (Revelation 5:8). And again – *To him who sits on the* **throne** *and to the Lamb be praise and honour and glory and power, for ever and ever!* (Revelation 5:13). Notice that they acknowledged God (the Lamb) as the Sovereign Lord, on the Throne. Why do we argue with God when He is the King! No one can tell God what to do. We can entreat Him, but never command Him.

They bowed, or fell down

*the twenty-four elders **fall down** before him who sits on the throne, and worship him who lives for ever and ever* (Revelation 4:10). And again – *The four living creatures said, 'Amen,' and the elders **fell down** and worshipped* (Revelation 5:14). Once more – *All the angels were standing around the throne and around the elders and the four living creatures. They fell down on their faces before the throne and worshipped God* (Revelation 7:11). Notice that the angels crowd round the throne because they don't want to miss anything going on there. They are all worshipping the King of all kings – the One who will reign for ever and ever – *The seventh angel sounded his trumpet, and there were loud voices in heaven, which said: 'The kingdom of the world has become the **kingdom** of our Lord and of his Christ, and he will **reign** for ever and ever'* (Revelation 11:15). In fact they are seeing the start of the new things which God is bringing about in Heaven – *saying: 'We give thanks to you, Lord God Almighty, the One who is and who was, because you have taken your great power and **have begun to reign***' (Revelation 11:17). Interestingly, bowing or falling down is one of the most common aspects of worship in the Bible. How different today! Worship is often mentioned after times of judgement too!

'Proskuneo', is a Greek word meaning 'to bow down', or 'to reverently draw near to kiss'. This is what the wise men did – *and asked, 'Where is the one who has been born king of the Jews? We saw his star in the east and have come to **worship** him.' ... On coming to the house, they saw the child with his mother Mary, and they **bowed down** and **worshipped** him. Then they opened their treasures and presented him with gifts of gold and of incense and of myrrh* (Matthew 2:2 & 11). To bow down and to fall down are roughly the same thing.

Think about this incident in the Bible – *Now when Joshua was near Jericho, he looked up and saw a man standing in front of him with a drawn sword in his hand. Joshua went up to him and asked, 'Are you for us or for our enemies?' 'Neither,' he replied, 'but as commander of the army of the*

LORD *I have now come.'* Then Joshua *fell face down to the
ground in reverence, and asked him, 'What message does my
Lord have for his servant?'* (Joshua 5:13, 14). Joshua was
rather proud after his victories in warfare, but when he saw
the great angel (probably Jesus in fact), He suddenly realised that he was facing God, or God's messenger. He then
rapidly bowed before the Lord. This attitude needs to be
more common in today's church as we reverently draw near
to God in our worship times. The Psalmists knew a lot
about reverence, and they practised it. *But I, by your great
mercy, will come into your house; in* **reverence** *will I bow
down toward your holy temple* (Psalm 5:7). Why have we
lost the habit in the 'free' churches? Is it because we have
become careless? Or over familiar with Almighty God? So
then, bowing down, awe, holiness, and fear are essential in
worship. Such things are seen in the Bible. So reverence and
kneeling down are aspects of worship. The church has lost
the habit of bowing down before God, bearing in mind that
bowing needs to be an attitude of heart as much as physically kneeling down before Him. Let David exhort us in his
words – *Come, let us* **bow down** *in worship, let us* **kneel** *before
the* LORD *our Maker* (Psalm 95:6).

Yet another Greek word worth looking at is *'sebomai'* –
meaning 'having a sense of awe'. There is no doubt that we
will all be awestruck in Heaven as we see the unfolding of
God's plans for the eternal future. The fact that there is so
much bowing down indicates that there will be awe in
Heaven. Awe was evident in the early church – *Everyone
was filled with* **awe** ... (Acts 2:43). *When the crowd saw this,
they were filled with* **awe;** *and they praised God, who had
given such authority to men* (Matthew 9:8). *Therefore, since
we are receiving a kingdom that cannot be shaken, let us be
thankful, and so worship God acceptably with reverence and*
awe, *for our 'God is a consuming fire'* (Hebrews 12:28, 29).
Whenever God works in power or revival, there is a sense
of awe about. We should look for it as a proof that out
periods of 'blessing' are indeed of God. If there is only

exuberance, or even if there is only phenomena, there is reason to doubt that what we see is a true work of God.

Reverential fear is another characteristic of Heaven. None of us should ever become so familiar with God that we forget to reverence Him. Here on earth godly fear is an aspect of awe, and it often comes about when God is judging His people. Perhaps that is why the UK is heading for even greater judgement, so that godly fear and the honour of God's name will be restored among us. The angel exhorted the listeners to be in awe of God – let us hear his message today – *He said in a loud voice, 'Fear God and give him glory, because the hour of his judgment has come. Worship him who made the heavens, the earth, the sea and the springs of water'* (Revelation 14:7). No one should become over familiar with God. We can – . . . *approach the* **throne of grace** *with confidence* (Hebrews 4:16), but we must not approach God cheekily.

Holiness

Another Greek word is *'eusebeo'*, meaning 'piety' or 'holiness'. Holiness is the atmosphere of heaven. Holiness is not dullness; it is a refreshing, clean, beautiful attitude of heart which makes it a pleasure to be with. It is God's own nature. Being holy is an aspect of worship. We realise how holy God is, and we desire to be more like Him, and we know how He loves holiness, so, we make sure that we come before Him clean and ready to look into His face and offer Him our praises. Just as they did in Heaven – *Each of the four living creatures had six wings and was covered with eyes all around, even under his wings. Day and night they never stop saying: 'Holy, holy, holy is the Lord God Almighty, who was, and is, and is to come'* (Revelation 4:8). (Read Isaiah chapter 6 too.) These *living creatures* may be the Seraphim; if so, are they Heaven's worship leaders? David reminds us of God's holiness – *Exalt the Lord our God and worship at his footstool; he is* **holy** (Psalm 99:5). Other Scriptures mention it – *ascribe to the Lord the glory due his name. Bring an offering and come before him; worship the Lord in the splendour of his*

holiness (1 Chronicles 16:29). God plainly commands us to –
be holy. He gives us a reason for being holy – **be holy,**
because I am holy (1 Peter 1:14–16). Like Father, like child.
True or false? Holiness must be seen in our hearts, and in
what we do – **be holy in all you do** (1 Peter 1:16). It is when
we see something of the holiness of God that we are likely to
worship Him in depth and reality. Isaiah certainly did. God
grant us similar visions, and similar results. Bear in mind
though that Isaiah probably prophesied through scarred
lips for the rest of his life!

Silence

In Heaven, we **are** in the presence of God, and I do not
believe that we will be vocal all the time. As the prophet said
– *But the LORD is in his holy temple; let all the earth be silent*
before him (Habakkuk 2:20). There was at least one time of
silence in Heaven – *When he opened the seventh seal, there*
was silence in heaven for about half an hour (Revelation 8:1).
It seems to have occurred during a time when the sufferings
of the martyrs were being reviewed, and there eternal blessing was being promised. It was also just before the prayers
of the saints were being surveyed. I can imagine it being an
awesome occasion as we see the way in which God had
enabled the martyrs to endure their sufferings. Then, as the
record of all the heart cries from God's people through the
ages is replayed, it would certainly cause Heaven to be still
in order to listen. It was possibly a worship time, if we
regard attentive silence as an aspect of worship.

There is not much of this attentive silence in today's
worship, except perhaps in the more traditional denomina-
tions. We do not have to be saying something all the time in
our sessions. Scripture says that there is – *a time to be silent*
and a time to speak (Ecclesiastes 3:7). I love those rare occasions when we are so focused on God, and so conscious of
His presence that we are lost for words. Our problem is that
we say too much. Words prevent worship. These times of
silence on earth usually come about when people are
sensing the presence of God. One thing is necessary though

to stop the mind from wandering during silence, and that is a focus. The focus in Heaven is God – who He is as well as what He has done; let us have the same focus down here.

This lack of silence down here might be due to the fact that many people cannot live without some kind of sound in the background. A non-Christian teenager said to me recently, 'I can't bear silence because if I did not have music playing I would have time to think, and I dare not think about the future.' How sad, but it is the same with many Christian young people – they cannot cope with silence. Many church leaders do not know how to cope with silence in their meetings. And as for some music groups, though certainly not all, they cannot cope with it at all. Even if there is a brief time of quiet, the musicians are likely to keep up their strumming during it. Bless them, why can't they keep quiet!

Everyone in Heaven was involved

There were no slackers in Heaven's meetings. Everyone was keen to glorify God. There should not be any lazy worshippers in our churches either. Our meetings are to help us to worship God and to praise Him, after all angels do so! – *Then I looked and heard the voice of many angels, numbering* **thousands upon thousands**, *and ten thousand times ten thousand. They encircled the throne and the living creatures and the elders. In a loud voice they sang: 'Worthy is the Lamb, who was slain, to receive power and wealth and wisdom and strength and honour and glory and praise!' Then I heard every creature in heaven and on earth and under the earth and on the sea, and all that is in them, singing* (Revelation 5:11–13). Are we going to let them outdo us? What does God get from you when you go to your meetings?

Worship need not be inhibited

Another Greek word proves that we need not be inhibited in our worship. It is the word *'methusko'* which literally means 'drunk'! *Do not get **drunk** on wine, which leads to debauchery. Instead, be **filled** (drunk) with the Spirit* (Ephesians 5:18). The Christians at Pentecost looked as though they were drunk, but they were truly worshipping God without inhibition, and He was certainly enjoying it – *All of them were filled with the Holy Spirit and began to speak in other tongues as the Spirit enabled them* (Acts 2:4). *Some, however, made fun of them and said, 'They have had too much wine'* (Acts 2:13). Well they would, wouldn't they! Worship in Heaven will be utterly uninihibited as well as reverent. Derived meanings of *drunk in the Spirit* would be uninhibited, or transported. Let us look at some of the indications of uninhibited worship.

Clapping their hands is a well understood way of showing approval on earth, it is also scriptural – *Clap your hands, all you nations; shout to God with cries of joy* (Psalm 47:1).

Shouting is fine as long it is for the right reason – *May those who delight in my vindication shout for joy and gladness; may they always say, 'The LORD be exalted, who delights in the well-being of his servant'* (Psalm 35:27). *In a **loud voice** they sang: 'Worthy is the Lamb, who was slain, to receive power and wealth and wisdom and strength and honour and glory and praise!'* (Revelation 5:12).

Leaping is fine too as long as there is a good reason. I have promised to leap and dance when my sick wife is healed. God says that we can do so – *Rejoice in that day and **leap for joy**, because great is your reward in heaven. For that is how their fathers treated the prophets* (Luke 6:23).

Lifting up hands in worship is biblical, although it must not be a mere habit – it should mean something – *Lift up your hands in the sanctuary and praise the LORD* (Psalm 134:2). Make sure our hands are clean – *Who may ascend the hill of the LORD? Who may stand in his holy place? He who has clean hands and a pure heart, who does not lift up his soul to an idol or swear by what is false* (Psalm 24:3–4).

Singing is a main way of worshipping God. They sing in Heaven – *And they sang a new song before the throne and before the four living creatures and the elders. No-one could* learn the song except the 144,000 who had been redeemed from the earth (Revelation 14:3). I believe that the 144,000 represent all those who are saved. I do not believe that these are only so called Jehovah's Witnesses. (These purveyors of heresy need to tremble before God for their evil doctrines.) David exhorts us to sing to God now, while we are on earth. *Sing to the LORD a new song, his praise in the assembly of the saints* (Psalm 149:1). Get some practice while you read this book, sing God a love song in your home.

Dancing is quite in order here and in Heaven – David **danced** before the Lord. *David, wearing a linen ephod, danced before the LORD with all his might* (2 Samuel 6:14). Will we be less joyful and exuberant in Heaven? Impossible!

Service is an aspect of worship

The Greek word *'latreuo'* means 'service as an aspect of worship'. It is used in the verse – *The throne of God and of the Lamb will be in the city, and his servants will **serve him*** (Revelation 22:3). Jesus used this word when He said – *Jesus said to him, 'Away from me, Satan! For it is written: "**Worship** the Lord your God, and **serve him** only."'* (Matthew 4:10). He combines worship and service using the same word *'latreuo'*.

Therefore what we **do** should be part of our worship. We cannot limit worship to what we experience together in our meetings – *And whatever you **do**, whether in word or **deed**, do it all in the name of the Lord Jesus, giving thanks to God the Father through him* (Colossians 3:17). This does away with the distinction sometimes made between spiritual activity and secular work. In God's eyes this distinction does not exist. I think that a good motto for us whatever we are doing or thinking, whether we are in meetings, or at our daily work, or working around the house would be – 'will this please Jesus?' If you work in a factory, and you do your work thoroughly, you are worshipping God. The same applies if you work in a shop, bank, school, dustcart, or palace. Service is an aspect of worship. They do it in heaven, we can do it on earth before we get there. Get some practice!

A major theme in Heaven's worship

Their songs had a godly theme – *And they sang a new song: 'You are worthy to take the scroll and to open its seals, because you were slain, and with your blood you purchased men for God from every tribe and language and people and nation'* (Revelation 5:9). Our redemption will be a major theme of our worship throughout eternity. Angels sing to God, and their theme is the salvation that God has given to us, and their praise to Jesus as the One who brought it about. The One who would not let them intervene at Calvary because we would never have been saved if He had. This great sacrifice will undoubtedly inspire our worship forever, for who could ever forget it? The first mention of worship in the Bible is in Genesis chapter 22, and it was in the context of tremendous sacrifice. Abram offered his beloved son Isaac to God, and I could imagine that his heart was breaking as he did so. There was a real cost to his worship of God, and this made it all the more acceptable to God, who appreciated the wholeheartedness of what he was doing. Scripture speaks about offering a **sacrifice** of praise – *Through Jesus, therefore, let us continually offer to God a **sacrifice of praise** – the fruit of lips that confess his name* (Hebrews 13:15). Let us make sure that there is reality and sacrifice in our worship. We may have to start with gritted teeth and in cold blood, but our teeth willl soon be ungritted, and our blood warmed! We need to take a long hard look at our worship to see whether it is just habitual mouthing of words, or mere enjoyment for us, or real worship of God. For example, I wonder what would happen if the words 'hallelujah' and 'amen' were banned for a while!

A major feature of Heaven's worship is thanksgiving – *Whenever the living creatures give glory, honour and **thanks** to him who sits on the throne and who lives for ever and ever*

(Revelation 4:9). We have so many things to thank God for; among them are –

Our great salvation

God saved us forever – millions of us – *And they sang a new song: 'You are worthy to take the scroll and to open its seals, because you were slain, and with your blood you **purchased men** for God from every tribe and language and people and nation* (Revelation 5:9).

No wonder that salvation will be a major reason for our worship – *And they cried out in a loud voice: 'Salvation belongs to our God, who sits on the throne, and to the Lamb'* (Revelation 7:10).

Our kingly position

This is something to thank God for – *You have made them to be a kingdom and priests to serve our God, and they will reign on the earth* (Revelation 5:10).

Our cleanness

Surely we are glad to be clean enough to live in Heaven; He has made us clean enough to live with Him in His holiness forever – *After this I looked and there before me was a great multitude that no one could count, from every nation, tribe, people and language, standing before the throne and in front of the Lamb. They were wearing **white robes** and were holding palm branches in their hands* (Revelation 7:9). *And they cried out in a loud voice: 'Fine linen, bright and clean, was given her to wear.' (Fine linen stands for **the righteous acts of the saints**.)* (Revelation 19:8). The King James version puts it this way – *And to her was granted that she should be arrayed in fine linen, clean and white: for the fine linen is the **righteousness** of saints* (Revelation 19:8 KJV). I quote it because it is worth bearing in mind that we do righteous acts because God has given us the righteousness of His Son. Scripture points this out – *It is because of him that you are in Christ Jesus, who has become for us wisdom from God – that is, our righteousness, holiness and redemption* (1 Corinthians 1:30).

Our earthly blessings

These include blessings such as food, clothing, homes, money, and safety. There is so much to give thanks to God for; have you thanked Him today for all your blessings as Scripture exhorts us? – *Praise the LORD, O my soul, and forget not all his benefits* (Psalm 103:2).

Worship on earth today

Let me say first of all that I love worship, and I need it. I love most of our major worship leaders and groups, but I am seriously worried about the way that some of them are influencing and even directing our churches. The world's music groups are being copied to an alarming extent in some of the Fellowships.

Thank God for those wonderful times of true worship that we have seen in the past years. When I was baptised in the Spirit in 1960, worship was not a strong point, in fact it was often dull and uninspired. But the Holy Spirit brought worship to life for many of us, and we even got excited sometimes! Many churches whose worship had been dominated for years by the choir or the organist suddenly experienced new liberty and new forms of worship. Out went many organs, and in came many guitars. Please remember that many church organists were godly and spiritual people, and many choirs really did honour God with their singing, but many did not.

Alas, blessing fades, and habit takes over. Much of today's worship is unreal, and untruthful. In many of the New churches there is an automatic format – a new 'liturgy'. Meetings are nearly always introduced as 'A time of worship', which usually means anything up to an hour or more of singing. This is often followed by 'singing with the Spirit'. This is not necessarily bad, but if it becomes a ritual, there is reason to deny that it is real worship. We are in great danger of regarding this item in the programme as warming up time for the lazy Christians who have come unprepared to worship the living God, or as an aspect of entertainment for bored Christians. Shoddy offerings do not please or glorify God. Malachi rebuked the priests for bringing such offerings, and he questioned whether God would accept them. By the way, real worship will leave time for preaching, and for digesting what has been said from the Scriptures.

Thank God for most of the composers and musicians we have to day (and I am one of those who need the good ones). Yet, we do give God some shoddy offerings, often through some trigger happy guitarist dominating the meeting from the vantage point of a powerful amplification system, or through a 'performance' by the musicians or leader, or through songs containing unsound doctrine, bad grammar, sentimentality, triumphalism, and mere repetition. Worship does not glorify God unless it is under the inspiration of the Holy Spirit. But all is not lost! We can praise God for the increasing number of singers and musicians who are praying over their music more than they did, and meditating on the Scriptures to a greater degree. Men and women who want to raise the standard of worship so that it resembles that in Heaven. God bless them! When we get to Heaven we will **not** be unprepared to worship God. One reason being that we will be able to see Him. Perhaps one reason for shoddy worship on earth is that there is little which reveals God in our meetings. Paul said – ... *what good will I be to you, unless I bring you some revelation or knowledge or prophecy or word of instruction?* (1 Corinthians 14:6). Seeing that revelation helps to prevent shoddy worship, we should covet it earnestly.

Can we learn anything from Heaven's worship?

So can we learn anything from Heaven's worship where they always get it right? I say – Yes.

Get the focus right

All the focus was on God. No individual stood out – (no one was even standing up!). No worship leader, nor singer, nor musician took centre stage in Heaven – only God did. We can learn to make sure that we have no mere performers in our worship groups today. The church should have no superstars, whether they are musicians or preachers. By the way, the focus must not be primarily on our blessings, but on the One who brought them to us.

Let the musicians be servants not directors

The worship group and or musicians are servants – no more, and no less. They should be a group who serve the church, especially the church leaders when they are required to do so. Church leaders should lead church meetings, not the worship group. If this is not the case, then it is quite likely that the meetings, are directed by the group and not the God-appointed leaders. I am not sure about the scriptural basis for today's 'worship leaders'.

Come prepared

Let the congregation come to church prepared in heart to worship. Then they will not need to warmed up as TV audiences are. It is good for leaders to have an agenda for meetings, but they must hold it lightly in case it is not the same as God's agenda. Let us come with vision and revelation to help our worship. That is one reason why we need such gifts. In Heaven they see God face to face, so they have the advantage over us here on earth. They find no difficulty in worshipping God. However, we can ask God to give us more revelation, and then we may not have such a problem in worship.

Give God time to speak

Most good worship comes out of meetings which include periods of quiet in which we can hear God clearly. If we have compulsive prophesiers, we must restrain them so that we can listen in peace. Those who prophesy best are those who spend much time listening to God. Let them speak indeed, but again when it is the right moment.

Avoid jargon and lies

Some of the old hymns were spoiled by sentimentalism or pious jargon – but so are some of our modern songs. Bad grammar, silly phrases, and bad rhyming are some of the things which offend the Holy Spirit. We also sing plenty of lies. For example when we sing 'We are more than conquerors...'. Is it true? None of the words used in heaven's worship are crude, silly, or untrue. Their songs are not meaningless.

Musical instruments in Heaven

We don't find too many references to musical instruments in Heaven except for harps – *And when he had taken it, the four living creatures and the twenty-four elders fell down before the Lamb. Each one had a harp* (Revelation 5:8), and trumpets. Trumpets are mentioned in Revelation 8:7–13, and in chapters 9 and 10. They seem to manage with less than we do! Even the trumpets seemed to be used mainly to herald the announcements! There is some reference to the use of instruments on earth – *Praise him with the sounding of the trumpet, praise him with the harp and lyre, praise him with tambourine and dancing, praise him with the strings and flute, praise him with the clash of cymbals, praise him with resounding cymbals. Let everything that has breath praise the* LORD. *Praise the* LORD (Psalm 150:3–6). The latter verse probably includes the bagpipes!

But can we do without instruments in our worship today? Probably not, although we spend a phenomenal amount of money on them, to say nothing of the trade in PA equipment. Whether it is justified is something which church leaders should think about. I think it is good when we have godly musicians who play 'in the Spirit', and I confess that I love music, and I have no objection to instruments. In fact, when I get to Heaven I hope to find all kinds of instruments, and I would like to be able to play them all. Let us just be careful that we keep the spirit of the world out of our music, worship, and spending. John Wesley spoke to thousands without a microphone, so perhaps it is possible for us to do likewise! The worship in Heaven will be wonderful, and we will not need so much paraphernalia there. With our new bodies we will have new voices, and we will all be in harmony. What a wonderful prospect. May the Holy Spirit help us to be those *true worshippers* [who] *will worship the Father in spirit and truth* on the earth so that we are ready to join in the songs of the redeemed.

Angels do worship God, but their worship includes their activities. Let us find out more about them . . .

Chapter 13

Activities of Angels

Angels are not divine, for they are created beings. They are
very powerful, but they are not **all** powerful. Only God is
Almighty. They are not everywhere at once because only
God is omnipresent. There seem to be different kinds of
angelic beings, and they may be in a kind of hierarchy. The
Bible speaks of angels, and **great** angels, but there is no
point in labouring the distinction. The main thing is that
they serve God and they serve us, His people. The descriptions include the following –

Cherubim

*While I watched, the cherubim spread their wings and rose
from the ground ... They stopped at the entrance to the east
gate of the Lord's house, and the glory of the God of Israel
was above them. These were the living creatures I had seen
beneath the God of Israel by the Kebar River, and I realised
that they were cherubim. Each had four faces and four wings,
and under their wings was what looked like the hands of a man*
(Ezekiel 10:19–21).

The writer to the Hebrews described one of their func-
tions during Israel's wanderings – *Above the ark were the
cherubim of the Glory*... (Hebrews 9:5).

Seraphim

Above him were **seraphs**, *each with six wings: With two wings they covered their faces, with two they covered their feet, and with two they were flying* (Isaiah 6:2). These may be the same as the 'Living Creatures' in – *Each of the four* **living creatures** *had six wings and was covered with eyes all around, even under his wings. Day and night they never stop saying: 'Holy, holy, holy is the Lord God Almighty, who was, and is, and is to come'* (Revelation 4:8).

A Seraph applied the cleansing fire to Isaiah the prophet's lips – *Then one of the* **seraphs** *flew to me with a live coal in his hand, which he had taken with tongs from the altar. With it he touched my mouth and said, 'See, this has touched your lips; your guilt is taken away and your sin atoned for'* (Isaiah 6:6–7).

The Cherubim and Seraphim do not **guard** the Throne of God, they **attend** it. God does not need guarding, for He is unassailable.

Rulers and Authorities

The Bible mentions these rulers in the verse which declares the Lordship of Jesus over them all – *far above all rule and authority, power and dominion, and every title that can be given, not only in the present age but also in the one to come* (Ephesians 1:21). I believe that these rulers are both good and evil. The devil has some of his rulers in the heavenly place, but God has far more of His rulers, and they are more than a match for the devil's army. It is salutary to realise that they all watch us to see if we are leading godly lives.

Archangels

These may be among the good Rulers mentioned above – *For the Lord himself will come down from heaven, with a loud command, with the voice of the* **archangel** *and with the trumpet call of God, and the dead in Christ will rise first*

(1 Thessalonians 4:16). The verse mentions **the** archangel, inferring that there is only one, who seems to be Michael – *But even the* **archangel** *Michael, when he was disputing with the devil about the body of Moses, did not dare to bring a slanderous accusation against him, but said, 'The Lord rebuke you!'* (Jude 1:9). Michael seems to be the leader of the armies of Heaven, although he is himself under the Lordship of Jesus. He fought on the one occasion in Heaven – *And there was* **war in heaven.** **Michael and his angels fought** *against the dragon, and the dragon and his angels fought back* (Revelation 12:7). And he fought in the Heavenly places – *But the prince of the Persian kingdom resisted me twenty-one days. Then* **Michael,** *one of the* **chief princes,** *came to help me, because I was detained there with the king of Persia* (Daniel 10:13). He seems to be the particular guardian of the Jewish people – *but first I will tell you what is written in the Book of Truth. (No one supports me against them except Michael,* **your prince** *. . .)* (Daniel 10:21). Another reference is – *At that time Michael, the great prince who protects* **your people,** *will arise. There will be a time of distress such as has not happened from the beginning of nations until then. But at that time your people – everyone whose name is found written in the book – will be delivered* (Daniel 12:1).

Gabriel

Gabriel seems to be one of the chief angels, being entrusted with important errands for God, such as the announcement of the Coming of Jesus for the first time – *The angel answered, 'I am Gabriel.* **I stand in the presence of God,** *and I have been sent to speak to you and to tell you this good news'* (Luke 1:19). He also appeared on a critical occasion to Daniel to bring Divine revelation – *And I heard a man's voice from the Ulai calling, 'Gabriel, tell this man the meaning of the vision'* (Daniel 8:16); *while I was still in prayer, Gabriel, the man I had seen in the earlier vision, came to me* **in swift flight** *about the time of the evening sacrifice* (Daniel 9:21). Distance was no object!

Mighty angels

I hesitate to suggest that some angels might be stronger than others, but the verse here does speak about 'mighty' angels. *And I saw a **mighty angel** proclaiming in a loud voice, 'Who is worthy to break the seals and open the scroll?'* (Revelation 5:2). There is another reference to a mighty angel, but it might be the Lord Jesus who is in view – *Then I saw another **mighty** angel coming down from heaven. He was robed in a cloud, with a rainbow above his head; **his face was like the sun**, and his legs were like fiery pillars* (Revelation 10:1). I can't help thinking of the other verse – *In his right hand he held seven stars, and out of his mouth came a sharp double-edged sword. **His face was like the sun** shining in all its brilliance* (Revelation 1:16).

The angel of the Lord

Some references to *The angel of the Lord* could be a description of Jesus as He appeared on the earth on some occasions before His Advent. Some of these occasions are – *There the **angel of the LORD** appeared to him in flames of fire from within a bush. Moses saw that though the bush was on fire it did not burn up. So Moses thought, 'I will go over and see this strange sight – why the bush does not burn up.' When the LORD saw that he had gone over to look, **God** called to him from within the bush, 'Moses! Moses!' And Moses said, 'Here I am'* (Exodus 3:2–4).

*The **angel of the LORD** found Hagar near a spring in the desert; it was the spring that is beside the road to Shur* (Genesis 16:7). *She gave this name to **the LORD** who spoke to her: 'You are the **God** who sees me,' for she said, 'I have now seen the One who sees me'* (Genesis 16:13).

*When the **angel of the LORD** did not show himself again to Manoah and his wife, Manoah realized that it was **the angel of the LORD**. 'We are doomed to die!' he said to his wife. 'We have seen God!'* (Judges 13:21–22).

There are innumerable angels

There were 12 legions of angels (about 72,000) waiting to rescue Jesus from the Cross – *Do you think I cannot call on my Father, and he will at once put at my disposal more than* ***twelve legions*** *of angels?* (Matthew 26:53). So, how many more are there? The Bible says that there were – ... *many angels, numbering thousands upon thousands, and ten thousand times ten thousand. They encircled the throne and the living creatures and the elders* (Revelation 5:11). A verse in Hebrews indicates that there were many angels – *But you have come to Mount Zion, to the heavenly Jerusalem, the city of the living God. You have come to thousands upon thousands of angels in joyful assembly* (Hebrews 12:22).

A vision of angels

The Bible says that God will give visions to His people – *And afterwards, I will pour out my Spirit on all people. Your sons and daughters will prophesy, your old men will dream dreams, your young men will see visions* (Joel 2:28). I believe His Word, and I have asked Him for visions, and He has given them to me. So, we can safely share them without appearing to boast – they are after all gifts, not attainments. One of the visions granted to me is as follows: I saw a vast company of angels – so vast that they seemed to be arrayed in armies as though they were the rays of the sun. I could not see the end of each army because they seemed to stretch beyond the edge of space. All the angels were tall, very powerful looking, intelligent, and with glowing faces. As I looked at them, a great angel came towards me (I wonder if he was an archangel). He seemed to be concerned in case I was giving them too much attention. He said to me 'our power is great power. Through it, at the command of God we raise up empires, and at His word we cast them down. We carry out the command of God throughout Creation. But the power we have is only derived power given to us by God who is the all powerful One. Our faces do glow as you have seen, but the glow is only reflected glory, given by the One upon the Throne. Come now and worship the One who alone deserves worship.' Then, in the vision we went to kneel down before God the Father on the Throne. God then said to me 'I am your Father, I conceived the plan of salvation through which you have become my child. I welcomed you into My family and you will be in it forever. I am with you and I am for you. But turn now to My Son who is equal in power and deity – worship Him.' So I turned to Jesus and knelt before Him, and heard Him say 'I am your Saviour; I destroyed everything which barred your way into the Kingdom. I rose from the dead in glory with My foot firmly upon the neck of your enemy and mine. Remember that I am with you, and I am for you. Turn now to the Holy Spirit who is equal in power and deity – worship Him.' So I turned and knelt before the Holy Spirit and I heard Him say 'I am the One who brought you the gift of salvation, I drew you, convicted you, and changed you forever. I am the One who promised you all you need to follow the Son of God, and to be with your Father forever. I am with you, and I am for you.' Then it seemed that the great angel, and all the other angels, joined their voices with the voices of the Father, the Son, and the Holy Spirit and they all said to us in the church 'Never be afraid because we are with you, and we are for you.' I found it most comforting.

All angels are servants

We must not worship them. Some early Christians fell into the trap of doing so, despite the warning – *Do not let anyone who delights in false humility and the **worship of angels** disqualify you for the prize. Such a person goes into great detail about what he has seen, and his unspiritual mind puffs him up with idle notions* (Colossians 2:18). In Heaven they were very quick to warn John not to worship them – *At this I fell at his feet to worship him. But he said to me, 'Do not do it! I am a fellow servant with you and with your brothers who hold to the testimony of Jesus. **Worship God!** For the* *testimony of Jesus is the spirit of prophecy'* (Revelation 19:10).

We judge Angels!

Do you not know that we will judge angels? How much more the things of this life! (1 Corinthians 6:3). The word 'judge' can mean ordain, esteem, determine, punish, or condemn. In chapter 11 – 'The Judgement Seat of Christ', I mention the fact that we will be with God when He judges (punishes and condemns) the fallen angels, so in that sense we will judge fallen angels. But I have a feeling (but I am not quite sure) that we will rule over them in the Kingdom. Perhaps they will carry out our plans in our particular aspect of the Kingdom? At the moment, in the words of Scripture, we are – . . . *a little lower than the angels*; yet later the verse says of God *you crowned him with glory and honor* (Hebrews 2:7). If the word 'him' refers to man, then we will be superior to, or over the angels, thus determining what they do. Of course we ourselves will always be subject to the authority of God, but we will be very great people in His Kingdom. Great enough to rule over angels. Never forget the sheer nobility of our calling!

Angels worship in Heaven

They worship God and rejoice before Him – *All the angels were **standing around the throne** and around the elders and the four living creatures. They fell down on their faces before the throne and **worshipped** God* (Revelation 7:11).

They are absorbed in what God is doing whether it is in Heaven, or on earth – *It was revealed to them that they were not serving themselves but you, when they spoke of the things that have now been told you by those who have preached the gospel to you by the Holy Spirit sent from heaven. Even **angels long to look into these things*** (1 Peter 1:12). God allows all kinds of things to happen to us so that He can use us as a demonstration of His love, grace, and power.

131

Consider the Scripture – *His intent was that now, through the church, the manifold wisdom of God should be made known to the rulers and authorities in the heavenly realms* (Ephesians 3:10). This is the only Scripture to make sense to my wife and I through all the years of our disabilities. At least God was getting a demonstration from us, and that is worth everything. Paul said rather wryly – *For it seems to me that God has put us apostles on display at the end of the procession, like men condemned to die in the arena. We have been made a spectacle to the whole universe, to angels as well as to men* (1 Corinthians 4:9). Angels worship God when they see us soul-winning – *In the same way, I tell you, there is **rejoicing** in the presence of the angels of God over one sinner who repents* (Luke 15:10).

Angels prophesied to John in Heaven

Then the angel said to me: 'Why are you astonished? I will explain to you the mystery of the woman and of the beast she rides, which has the seven heads and ten horns'. The beast, which you saw, once was, now is not, and will come up out of the Abyss and go to his destruction. The inhabitants of the earth whose names have not been written in the book of life from the creation of the world will be astonished when they see the beast, because he once was, now is not, and yet will come (Revelation 17:7, 8).

Angels also operate on earth

They serve us

*Are not all angels ministering spirits sent to **serve** those who will inherit salvation?* (Hebrews 1:14).

They are often in disguise – *Do not forget to entertain strangers, for by so doing some people have **entertained angels** without knowing it* (Hebrews 13:2).

They guard us

By guarding our little ones – *See that you do not look down on one of these little ones. For I tell you that **their angels** in heaven **always see the face** of my Father in heaven* (Matthew 18:10).

They rescue us

The angel of the LORD *encamps around those who fear him, and he **delivers** them* (Psalm 34:7).

Paul and Silas were rescued – *But during the night an angel of the Lord opened the doors of the jail and brought them out* (Acts 5:19).

Peter was rescued – *Then the angel said to him, 'Put on your clothes and sandals.' And Peter did so. 'Wrap your cloak around you and follow me,' the angel told him* (Acts 12:8).

None of my experiences can match those of the Apostles, and we must not say too much about them. However, we can encourage each other to some degree, and that is why I include one or two of them here. I used to drive a heavy truck, and on one occasion I was driving down a hill with a heavy load of steel on board. The road was very busy as I approached a roundabout. As I put my foot on the brake, it went straight down to the floor. Although I wrestled with the gearstick and tried to bump the truck against the kerb I went faster and faster down towards the busy intersection. I cried to God, and then careered round and round the roundabout. Suddenly I felt strong hands on mine helping me to steer the truck round and round the island. Then I came to a stop, and it was only then that I realised that it was humanly impossible to do such a thing, and what is more, the 30 tons of steel had not shifted at all! I have no doubt at all that angels saved my life. On another occasion while I was a city Missioner, I was preaching to some men in a cellar. Most of them were crazed with drink, and some were fighting with broken bottles and lumps of wood. Suddenly two of them came at me aiming for my eyes with the broken bottles. I was scared, and cried out 'Jesus, your angels please'. The bottles stopped within a inch of my eyes and the men stood there paralysed. I took the bottles out of their hands, and they then went and sat down quietly. Thank God for angels. Many missionaries could tell us far more than I have, but I want to thank God for His safety, and I want to encourage my readers to believe in the ministry of angels.

They supply our needs

Then he lay down under the tree and fell asleep. All at once an angel touched him and said, 'Get up and eat'. He looked around, and there by his head was a cake of bread baked over hot coals, and a jar of water. He ate and drank and then lay down again (1 Kings 19:5, 6).

They supplied the needs of Jesus – *Then the devil left him, and angels came and attended him* (Matthew 4:11). Jesus was a man as well as being God. He got tired, and expended great energy in His work on earth. In this colossal struggle against all the wiles of the wicked one, He was utterly victorious, but He was exhausted. So His Father sent a great angel to help Him to recover. Later on in the Garden of Gethsemane, Jesus prayed so hard, and with such intensity, that he was virtually bleeding – *An angel from heaven appeared to him and strengthened him. And being in anguish, he prayed more earnestly, and his* **sweat was like drops of blood** *falling to the ground* (Luke 22:43, 44). I believe that the Atonement was virtually accomplished in Gethsemane, even though it was not actually accomplished till Jesus' death on Calvary, but think what it took out of Him! He needed the angels to minister to Him, and they did!

Angels bring messages to us

For if the message **spoken by angels** *was binding, and every violation and disobedience received its just punishment* (Hebrews 2:2). *The angel of the LORD gave this charge to Joshua: 'This is what the LORD Almighty says: "If you will walk in my ways and keep my requirements, then you will*

*govern my house and have charge of my courts, and I will give
you a place among these standing here.'' '* (Zechariah 3:6–7).
*In the sixth month, God sent the angel Gabriel to Nazareth, a
town in Galilee, to a virgin pledged to be married to a man
named Joseph, a descendant of David. The virgin's name was
Mary. The angel went to her and said, 'Greetings, you who
are highly favoured! The Lord is with you'* (Luke 1:26–28).

Angels prophesied on earth

Before Jesus was born – *You will be with child and give birth
to a son, and you are to give him the name Jesus* (Luke 1:31).
And again when Jesus was in danger of death – *When they
had gone, an angel of the Lord appeared to Joseph in a dream.
'Get up,' he said, 'take the child and his mother and escape to
Egypt. Stay there until I tell you, for Herod is going to search
for the child to kill him'* (Matthew 2:13).

Angels prophesied to a soldier who was seeking for God
– *One day at about three in the afternoon he had a vision. He
distinctly saw an angel of God, who came to him and said,
'Cornelius!'. Cornelius stared at him in fear. 'What is it,
Lord?' he asked. The **angel answered**, 'Your prayers and gifts
to the poor have come up as a memorial offering before God'*
(Acts 10:3, 4).

Angels bring God's judgement on Earth

On earth, in earlier times the angels of God were enforcing
His judgements on mankind. David had sinned badly, and
God had no option but to punish him and the nation. But
notice the mercy of God as well as His judgement – *When
the angel stretched out his hand to destroy Jerusalem, the
LORD was grieved because of the calamity and said to the
angel who was afflicting the people, 'Enough! Withdraw your
hand.' The angel of the LORD was then at the threshing floor
of Araunah the Jebusite* (2 Samuel 24:16).

When evil rulers rose up against God's chosen nation
Israel, He sometimes allowed them a measure of victory as

a punishment for His erring nation, but, if they went too far, God intervened by sending great angels to deal with the cruel enemy – *And the* LORD *sent an angel, who annihilated all the fighting men and the leaders and officers in the camp of the Assyrian king. So he withdrew to his own land in disgrace. And when he went into the temple of his god, some of his sons cut him down with the sword* (2 Chronicles 32:21).

Proud king Herod spoke to his people and – *They shouted, 'This is the voice of a god, not of a man'* (Acts 12:22). He enjoyed it and promptly gave way to pride. God saw it and dispatched an angel to judge him, and, *Immediately, because Herod did not give praise to God, an angel of the Lord struck him down, and he was eaten by worms and died* (Acts 12:23).

Angels assist God on Judgement Day

These events of the Day of Judgement were previewed to John in Heaven, although I believe that the actual event will take place in or from the Heavenly places – *Then the angel took the censer, filled it with fire from the altar, and hurled it on the earth; and there came peals of thunder, rumblings, flashes of lightning and an earthquake* (Revelation 8:5).

They separated the saved from the unsaved – *Another angel came out of the temple in heaven, and he too had a sharp sickle. Still another angel, who had charge of the fire, came from the altar and called in a loud voice to him who had the sharp sickle, 'Take your sharp sickle and gather the clusters of grapes from the earth's vine, because its grapes are ripe'. The angel swung his sickle on the earth, gathered its grapes and threw them into the great winepress of God's wrath* (Revelation 14:17–19).

Then in this highly pictorial vision John saw them calling all the judgemental forces of God to come and do their part – *And I saw an angel standing in the sun, who cried in a loud voice to all the birds flying in mid-air, 'Come, gather together for the great supper of God'* (Revelation 19:17).

Angels engage in warfare

Either in the Heavenlies or on the earth

On one occasion when Israel was being defeated in war, God used Elisha to help them. Elisha had a servant, who could only see the enemy all around them. So Elisha, the prophet prayed for him – *And Elisha prayed, 'O LORD, open his eyes so he may see.' Then the LORD opened the servant's eyes, and he looked and saw the hills full of horses and chariots of fire all around Elisha* (2 Kings 6:17). These forces were angels of God, who were sent to reassure him.

Warfare in the heavenly places

When Daniel saw the warfare going on in the heavenlies, he had conversations with the angels, including Michael. One angel said – ... *Do not be afraid, Daniel. Since the first day that you set your mind to gain understanding and to humble yourself before your God, your words were heard, and I have come in response to them. But the prince of the Persian kingdom resisted me twenty-one days. Then Michael, one of the chief princes, came to help me, because I was detained there with the king of Persia. Now I have come to explain to you what will happen to your people in the future, for the vision concerns a time yet to come* (Daniel 10:12–14). What a comfort for him to see how great the heavenly hosts are.

In John's preview of history

John saw a great angel imprison the devil in the last day – *And I saw an angel coming down out of heaven, having the key to the Abyss and holding in his hand a great chain* (Revelation 20:1).

Angels assist us in the Kingdom, a realm which we will now consider ...

Chapter 14

The Kingdom

I confess straightaway that I do not understand everything about the Kingdom of Heaven. Some say that it is the Millennium, but there are several theories about the Millennium to which I refer in Appendix 1. Other people say that the Millennium is what we are living through at the moment. I would have to declare myself as one who believes in a modified form of Pre-Millenialism, although I do not think we will escape the Tribulation. After all, many are in tribulation now. As the Chairman of a Chinese Mission, I hear heartrending stories of Christians being persecuted and executed for their faith. Then there is the problem of where Israel fits in. I love Israel, and have ministered often in that land, and I believe that God does have a special purpose for that nation. My conviction is that the word in Genesis is still relevant – *I will make you into a great nation and I will bless you; I will make your name great, and you will be a blessing. I will bless those who bless you, and whoever curses you I will curse; and all peoples on earth will be blessed through you* (Genesis 12:2, 3). I am not an ardent Christian Zionist, and I believe that the Israeli's need the same Gospel that we need. They are far from being a blameless nation, but we would do well to review the effects of 'cursing' Israel even in our own declining nation. I am happy to leave the question of Israel and the future purposes of God to those who have studied it thoroughly. Another question is whether the

Church is the Kingdom or not; this has been debated many times. I am not debating it here!

So then, because my stated aim in this book is to enthuse the people of God about Heaven, to warn them about the dangers of Hell, and to urge all of us to get on with preaching the Gospel, I will sidestep some of these questions and stick to what I am reasonably sure about. Other men, far better qualified than I am can help us over the difficult questions in their books. And I for one will be grateful to them.

In Matthew 5:3–20 Jesus mentions this phrase *The Kingdom of Heaven* a number of times, and refers to it as the place in which we will be with Him forever. The Kingdom of Heaven is difficult to describe in any one term because it is so vast and has so many aspects. God is omnipresent, and He cannot be limited to one particular place. On the other hand the Bible does speak of Heaven as a place. So, lest we get too complicated, I will use the terms 'Heaven', and 'Kingdom of Heaven' to include Heaven the location – God's Home, and the realm or domain which I understand as the new Heaven and a new Earth, including this present earth during the reign of Jesus on it. Together these are the realm of the rule and the activities of God throughout Creation and eternity. I use headings such as 'The Kingdom on this present earth – stage one', and 'stage two' simply to keep some kind of order in this chapter. I have already written about some of the events in Heaven in chapter 5 – 'What is Heaven Like?' In this chapter I am using the term 'The Kingdom of Heaven' to describe those Heavenly activities which seem to take place either on this earth when Jesus reigns on it, or in the New Earth, or in the New Heaven. We must not be afraid to think out the events in Heaven, but on the other hand we must not let our imagination run away with us so that we become unscriptural. For an example of my method of inference in this book I take a phrase in the verse – *But about the Son he says, 'Your throne, O God, will last for ever and ever, and **righteousness will be the sceptre of your kingdom'*** (Hebrews 1:8), and I infer from it the effects of righteous behaviour in the

Kingdom, and I then try to describe how that could work out when Jesus reigns, and how the opposite kind of behaviour will not exist in the Kingdom.

Whether Jesus rules on the present earth, or the New Earth, or on both, and whether I am right in regarding them all as the 'Kingdom of Heaven' is not my major concern. The point is that ... *we will be with the Lord forever* (1 Thessalonians 4:17). Where He is, we will be with Him. This is what I want to stress in this book. If we must distinguish the Old earth and the New earth, I believe that the 'Millennial' earth will be a foretaste of those on the New Earth. Picking up from the previous chapters, I believe that we, having served the Lord on the present earth by extending His Kingdom or rule on it, now proceed into the eternal events in Heaven. After the exhilarating events of the Second Coming, the Wedding, and the Judgement Seat of Christ, we ask what comes next? Is there anything else? I believe there is. Firstly, we are obviously involved in the present earth under the rule of King Jesus, then involved on the New Earth and Heaven, then in the eternal Kingdom. There will be an eternal season of activity, creativity, progress and fulfilment.

Now let us look at the word 'kingdom'.

Realm or domain

The word 'kingdom' in Greek (*'basileia'*) means a 'realm' or 'domain'. The realm or domain of the Kingdom of Heaven, where we will be forever with the Lord, God describes as –
... *your inheritance, the **kingdom** prepared for you since the creation of the world* (Matthew 25:34). God, in His Word has said – *you will receive a rich welcome into the **eternal kingdom** of our Lord and Saviour Jesus Christ* (2 Peter 1:11). The word 'domain' might be more commonly used than the word 'realm' in some areas of the world, so I will explain it. 'Domain' (from Latin *'Dominus'*, meaning 'Lord', or the 'dominant Lord'), might be described as 'the realm of God's Sovereign rule and activity in Creation throughout

eternity'. So if I use the word 'realm' I use it as synonymous with 'domain'.

Rule

The word 'kingdom' also means to 'rule'. Jesus will rule over all Creation, He will *rule them with an iron sceptre; . . . just as I have received authority from my Father* (Revelation 2:27). An iron sceptre is not a weapon, it is a straightedge; something like those used in an engineering factory to see if an edge or surface is true and accurate. It is the gauge by which everything is tested to see if it is according to the design. The rule (government) of Christ will be sharp and decisive when he rules over the nations – *Out of his mouth comes a sharp sword with which to strike down the nations. 'He will rule them with an iron sceptre'* (Revelation 19:15). The rule of God will be established by Jesus, and there will be no other rule or authority but His. No wonder that we Christians pray daily – *your kingdom come, your will be done on earth as it is in Heaven* (Matthew 6:10). When all God's Laws are obeyed without exception, there is peace, safety, and satisfaction.

The Kingdom on this present earth – stage one

I refer to this present earth on which you are reading this book – where the church is at the moment. I do not believe that the church is the Kingdom, but an aspect of the Kingdom. We as Christians obey the rule of God in our daily lives, and by doing so reveal the principles of the Kingdom. We serve God, by preaching the Gospel, and extending the rule of God in our areas, thus demonstrating to the heavenly powers what it is going to be like later on. God has His heroes and heroines on earth, consider some of them – *. . . Gideon, Barak, Samson, Jephthah, David, Samuel and the prophets, who through faith conquered kingdoms, administered justice, and gained what was promised; who shut the mouths of lions, quenched the fury of the flames, and escaped the edge of the sword; whose weakness was turned to* *strength; and who became powerful in battle and routed foreign armies* (Hebrews 11:32–34). Later on they, together with us will inherit and rule in the Kingdom.

The Kingdom on this present earth – stage two

There will be a total restoration of all things when Jesus reigns. I expect that will be on this earth, but I am open to the possibility that it will be on the new earth. This total Restoration is mentioned in the Bible – *He* (Jesus) *must remain in Heaven until the time comes for God to restore everything, as he promised long ago through his holy prophets* (Acts 3:21). This restoration means that there will be nothing left which is unreconciled to God. Let Scripture emphasise this again – ... *and through him to reconcile to himself all things, whether things on earth or things in Heaven, by making peace through his blood, shed on the cross* (Colossians 1:20). This time of reconciliation and restoration will be a time when there is only one Name glorified as the Bible says – *that at the name of Jesus every knee should bow, in Heaven and on earth and under the earth* (Philippians 2:10).

I believe that this is where the Millennial reign of Jesus comes in. Whether it is for a literal one thousand years is not something I argue about, although the Bible does mention the period – *Blessed and holy are those who have part in the first resurrection. The second death has no power over them, but they will be priests of God and of Christ and will reign with him for a thousand years* (Revelation 20:6). During this time God will show the world what He had in mind in the first place. A beautified earth, with nothing on it to spoil it. The earth will not cease to be part of the realm of God at that time for God will be on it, and Jesus is God. Later on when God brings in the New Heaven and the New Earth the same rule applies – God is in both. We cannot say that God is in the new Heaven, but not in the New Earth. He is in both. They are one realm really. The devil who spoiled this earth in the first place will be imprisoned so that he can do nothing to spoil it again while Jesus reigns over it with us. I quote the Bible again – *He seized the dragon, that ancient serpent, who is the devil, or Satan, and bound him for a thousand years. He threw him into the Abyss, and locked and sealed it over him, to keep him from deceiving the nations anymore until the thousand years were ended. After that, he must be set free for a short time* (Revelation 20:2–3). With him imprisoned, the world will flourish in righteousness. The Bible declares that Jesus will rule in righteousness – *But about the Son he says, 'Your throne, O God, will last for ever and ever, and righteousness will be the sceptre of your kingdom* (Hebrews 1:8). Some characteristics of **un**-righteousness are murder, greed, domination, envy, together with those which bring about fear and the like. Jesus will not allow anything like them to exist in the Kingdom. There will be no famines because earth is used wisely – no slag heaps – everything used cleanly – all shared out fairly, including money – all skills shared – no dictators – no rushing about – no pollution – nothing allowed which takes away peace – no wrong competitiveness on roads or markets or anywhere else. Oh the joy of being in an environment where there are none of these hideous things! Praise God, isn't it thrilling! I try to picture the conditions in the Kingdom by describing the effects on earth of things such as fear, misuse of money, greed, and then describing the opposite conditions.

No fear in the Kingdom

On earth darkness brings fear to many people. Women are afraid to walk along the street. Children imagine all kinds of terrors in the dark. Most crime is committed in the dark. Jesus said so – *men loved **darkness** instead of light because their deeds were evil* (John 3:19). Fear takes many forms. Fear of death, of dying, of sickness, of redundancy, of penury, fear of man as the Bible says – ***Fear of man** will prove to be a snare, but whoever trusts in the Lord is kept safe* (Proverbs 29:25).

These fears often paralyse activity. Some forms of it

make it impossible for people to go into crowded places. Other forms of fear such as claustrophobia causes terror to some if they get into confined places. However, none of these things will ever be in the Kingdom of Heaven. It is a 'fear free' environment. This lovely freedom from fear is pictured by the prophet when he was given a vision of Israel's future – *Every man will sit under his own vine and under his own fig tree, and* ***no one will make them afraid****, for the* LORD *Almighty has spoken* (Micah 4:4). All in Heaven, whether Jew or Gentile will be free from fear.

No war in the Kingdom

Wars are increasing, and the ferocity of them. More sophisticated weapons arrive daily in the world's arsenals. Billions of pounds are spent on them while whole nations starve. Jesus warned us that this would happen – *You will hear of* ***wars*** *and rumors of* ***wars****, but see to it that you are not alarmed. Such things must happen, but the end is still to come* (Matthew 24:6). But, Jesus will rule with total authority. Not only will He have authority, He will have the power to enforce it. As it says – *He will judge between many peoples and will settle disputes for strong nations far and wide. They will beat their swords into ploughshares and their spears into pruning hooks. Nation will not take up sword against nation, nor will they train for war anymore* (Micah 4:3). Wars are caused by all sorts of things. Power struggles among world leaders, so-called 'class wars', political rivalry, territorial disputes, and the pride with which Satan has infected so many men and women. But in the Kingdom, none of these things will exist.

Perfect peace

If there is no war, and if there is an absence of the attitudes which cause it – there will be peace. In the Kingdom this will be a characteristic of Jesus' rule. Remember that Jesus rules in righteousness, and Scripture speaks of its wonderful effects – *The fruit of righteousness will be peace; the effect of righteousness will be quietness and confidence forever* (Isaiah 32:17). This verse will be fulfilled because the One who rules over the whole Creation will be the – ... *Prince of Peace* (Isaiah 9:6). Peace is the opposite of war, so if there are not wars, there must be peace. How we long for peace in our time. At the moment there are 140 wars or disputes going on, millions of people are homeless because of them, and many die because crops are ravaged by the war. Genocide is on the increase, and man's inhumanity to man has never been so marked. As if wars are not enough, there are an increasing number of murderous gangs about in our cities destroying our peace and quiet. Terrorist organisations give opportunities for murderers to operate under a banner of so-called politics. Even the more legitimate protest groups are increasingly turning to violence to attain their aims. There is little peace in this world, and it will get worse, and Jesus spoke of the effects on many who are terrified by all the world's violence – *Men will faint from terror, apprehensive of what is coming on the world, for the heavenly bodies will be shaken* (Luke 21:26). But Jesus will come, and He will bring the peace we long for. Praise Him for it.

No limitations

After the restoration there will be no limitations in the Kingdom of Heaven. At present we live on this earth in a time and space environment; we are therefore limited in our travel, and hindered by time constraints. We are limited in what our minds can take in; limited by the need to eat and drink and sleep; limited in strength and energy, limited by our inability to speak in all the languages on earth. Some countries have no minerals such as iron, aluminium etc., so they are limited in what they can produce, so they have to import from elsewhere. Some countries are short of water and cannot produce crops. Other nations are limited by the difficult terrain or temperature in their land. But in the Kingdom of Heaven these limitations do not exist. Of course I am thinking and writing in terms that we understand here and now – my mind is still that of an inhabitant of earth. In the Kingdom things may be very different, and I may be found to be inaccurate in what I am writing now. But I don't mind repeating things which I have stressed in previous chapters, so I say again – I want to enthuse us about the next life – I want heaven in all its aspects to be more real to us than it is. That's why I write this book!

Fairness and justice

God loves fairness and justice. He said that righteousness would be characteristic of the Kingdom, which implies fairness and justice – *But in keeping with his promise we are looking forward to a new heaven and a new earth, the home of righteousness* (2 Peter 3:13). After all the King in the Kingdom is the One of whom it is written – *But about the Son he says, 'Your throne, O God, will last for ever and ever, and **righteousness** will be the sceptre of your kingdom* (Hebrews 1:8). A righteous, just and fair King, and a Kingdom to match! Hallelujah!

The Bible is full of references to these practices: *The King is mighty, he loves justice – you have established equity; in Jacob you have done what is just and right* (Psalm 99:4); *Woe to you, teachers of the law and Pharisees, you hypocrites! You give a tenth of your spices – mint, dill and cummin. But you have neglected the more important matters of the law – **justice**, mercy and faithfulness. You should have practised the latter, without neglecting the former* (Matthew 23:23); *I saw heaven standing open and there before me was a white horse, whose rider is called Faithful and True. With **justice** he judges and makes war* (Revelation 19:11). But the motto of this world is 'grab what you can, and hold on to it'. This is true of many though not all people on earth whether we talk about money, houses, possessions, power, or land.

One of the blessings in the Kingdom of Heaven will be fair shares for all. Of course there will be people in it who will be given more responsibility than others; for example those I referred to when dealing with 'Rewards' in chapter 11 – 'The Judgement Seat of Christ' – who are given ten cities to rule over as opposed to those who only have five. But the point is that there will be no mere possessiveness, or competing for eminence, or jealousy despite the differentiation which God ordains. God will rectify all the unfairness we see in this present world. At the moment there is great unfairness in the distribution of things. There are money men with far more money than necessary, those with too many possessions such as film stars and pop stars, then there are power drunk rulers who have far too much power in the world and who use it badly, There are landowners today with far more land than they need, food is not shared as it should be. But God set is going to set it all to rights in the Kingdom.

Money

I do not say that it is wrong to have money in this world, but I do question the stewardship of it by many greedy people. The Bible says that – the *love of money is a root of all kinds of evil. Some people, eager for money, have wandered from the faith and pierced themselves with many griefs* (1 Timothy 6:10). One of the world's greatest problems is debt, and one of the main causes is the system of interest used. God had no time for those whose main interest was in getting as much interest as they could irrespective of the suffering they caused. He points out that such people are unlikely to be in His holy place – *A psalm of David. LORD, who may dwell in your sanctuary? Who may live on your holy hill?'* (Psalm 15:1) ... (one) *who lends his money without usury and does not accept a bribe against the innocent* (Psalm 15:5). God seems to dislike the whole process of taking excessive interest – *In you men accept bribes to shed blood; you take usury and excessive interest and make unjust gain from your neighbours by extortion. And you have forgotten me, declares the Sovereign LORD* (Ezekiel 22:12). In the Kingdom we may not use money at all – perhaps people will gladly exchange goods instead? But if money is used, Jesus will ensure that all have what they need, and none will be allowed to monopolise the supply.

Possessions can be a blessing or a curse. There is nothing particularly wrong with possessions as long as the stewardship of them is right and fair. There are some people today who have many many possessions, but their stewardship is faulty. For example, how can it be right for some people to have several houses when so many others are homeless? Why should some have a dozen cars when millions do not have a bicycle? We hear of women with hundreds of dresses, and men with dozens of suits; but are they necessary I wonder? What a disparity there is on earth today, but it is not right to become envious, or cynical, or aggrieved about these injustices, and I am not – but my point is that in the Kingdom of Heaven everything on earth will be willingly shared, and rightly apportioned.

Power is often in the wrong hands, and is greatly abused in many parts of the world. We only have to look at some of this world's dictators to see what awful abuses they inflict on those whom they are supposedly caring for. But in the Kingdom all power will be in the hands of Jesus and there will be no dictators or abuse of power. Doubtless He will give power to us too but there will be no abuse of it by us and our concern will be for the well-being of everyone everywhere.

Land is not fairly shared out in this world. Some have vast estates while others have a few square feet of land with a hovel on it for a home. Some multinational companies have forced the inhabitants out of great swathes of land so that they can exploit the minerals in it. There are some nations who are determined to enlarge their territory by annexing land from a neighbouring country. Many wars are waged because of one nation or one person's greed for territory. But, in the Kingdom of God all land will be shared out in a fair manner. There will be plenty to share out too, although at the moment much land has been destroyed by over-grazing, over-mining, or being poisoned by chemicals. Some of the deserts of this world have been created by people who thoughtlessly cut down the trees and destroyed the water and oxygen supplied by them. So the earth dried up and vegetation disappeared. Incidentally those who blame God for famine should remember that he gave us the stewardship of the earth, and if we destroy the land, why should He be blamed? In the Kingdom land will be transformed as God said – *The desert and the parched land will be glad; the wilderness will rejoice and blossom. Like the crocus* (Isaiah 35:1).

Food

Those with new bodies will not need to eat and drink, but if food and drink bring satisfaction, I expect we will be capable of eating and drinking. *Jesus came, took the bread and gave it to them, and did the same with the fish* (John 21:13).

In Heaven there are food bearing trees – *down the middle of the great street of the city. On each side of the river stood the tree of life, bearing twelve crops of fruit, yielding its fruit every month. And the leaves of the tree are for the healing of the nations* (Revelation 22:2). They seem to be there for the benefit of the nations, who are not necessarily those who are born again.

Despite man's bad stewardship of this earth, it is still incredibly beautiful. Its rivers, forests, trees, flowers, and mountains are wonderful. Its oceans teem with myriad forms of life, and the tides and wave patterns are fascinating. If it is so beautiful now, what will it be like when Jesus has restored it? I can hardly wait to see. Incidentally, with our new bodies we will be impervious to drowning so we will be able to explore underwater without drowning. Someone is bound to remind me that the Bible says – *there was no longer any sea* (Revelation 21:1). But it does not say that there will not be lakes or rivers. What I am really trying to emphasise is the great freedom we will enjoy when we are with Him. If I am wrong, tell me when we get there! We will be able to climb mountains without slipping. We will be able to move between the earth and the heavens without the need for life support systems. Is this far fetched? Am I letting my imagination run away with me? I don't think so. As have already said our bodies are like the resurrection body of Jesus, so we will be capable of many of the things which He can do.

Let me just say a word about durability in our world with its passion for more and more things, and the practice in many industries of built-in obsolescence so that more and more things can be manufactured. Things do not seem to wear out in the Kingdom of Heaven. Jesus indicates that there are things which are durable in that realm – *... Provide purses for yourselves that will not **wear out**, a treasure in heaven that will **not be exhausted**, where no thief comes near and **no moth destroys*** (Luke 12:33). As I said in the Preface, we should be careful of taking things too literally. In this passage, I don't think that the purses are actual ones, but Jesus is explaining a principle, using common objects to do so. Here is another example – *But store up for yourselves treasures in heaven, where **moth and rust do not destroy**, and where thieves do not break in and steal* (Matthew 6:20). Jesus was not saying that there were moths and rust in the Kingdom, nor was He saying that there will be thieves be in the Kingdom. He was using the fact that there are thieves on earth **now** to point out how wonderful it will be to be without them then.

Best of all, Peter says that our inheritance in the Kingdom of heaven is durable – *and into an inheritance that can never perish, spoil or fade – kept in heaven for you* (1 Peter 1:4). It does not fade, it does not disappear, and it does not need constant renewing. We will not need the constant renewal of clothes. Neither men nor women will be disappointed by having no new clothes. We will be glorious enough anyway, and there will be so many other pleasures that we will not even think about clothes or whatever else give us pleasure to buy down here. It is interesting to note that God miraculously preserved the clothes of the Israelites in the wilderness – *... These forty years the LORD your God has been with* *you, and you have not lacked anything* (Deuteronomy 2:7). *Your clothes did not wear out and your feet did not swell during these forty years* (Deuteronomy 8:4). God did it then. He can do it in the Kingdom if He wants to.

There will be activity and service

Whether we think of this present earth when Jesus reigns over it, or the New Earth one thing is sure – there will be activity and service. There will be progress which implies purposeful, worthwhile activity. This will be an aspect of our life in the New Heaven. We need have no fear of being bored there. With God around there will be no lack of creative things to do. It is not possible to know exactly what our activities there will be, but Scripture gives us hints, and we can legitimately deduce some things from them. Just as we have been – *God's fellow workers* (2 Corinthians 6:1) on earth, so we will be working with Him in Heaven.

God enjoys working with us here, and seeing that He does not change, He will enjoy it in Glory too – *Therefore, 'they are before the throne of God and serve **him** day and night in his temple'* (Revelation 7:15). *No longer will there be any curse. The throne of God and of the Lamb will be in the city, and his servants will serve **him*** (Revelation 22:3).

Service will include Reigning

Jesus will reign over this present earth together with us. *Jesus said to them, 'I tell you the truth, at the renewal of all things, when the Son of Man sits on his glorious throne, you who have followed me will also sit on **twelve thrones**, judging the twelve tribes of Israel'* (Matthew 19:28). He may have been speaking on that occasion to His Jewish disciples, but another Scripture includes us as well – *You have made them to be a kingdom and priests to serve our God, and they will reign **on the earth*** (Revelation 5:10). The NIV blurs a distinction here, so I quote from another version – *And have made us **kings** and priests to our God; And we shall* *reign on the earth* (Revelation 5:10 NKJV). We will reign with Jesus as kings. God has made us kings or kingly. (The terms are masculine, but they embrace men and women. In any case gender will be unimportant in Heaven.) – *and (He) has made us **kings and priests** to His God and Father, to Him* be *glory and dominion forever and ever. Amen* (Revelation 1:6 NKJV). We seem to be kings forever – ... *And they will **reign for ever and ever*** (Revelation 22:5). Kings have power, they are rulers. The Greek word for 'king' means 'ruler'.

But **where** do we rule and reign? I cannot believe that we can be kings without a kingdom over which to reign. I do not know exactly what our kingdom will be, but I suggest some spheres in God's domain over which He may give us rule. Seeing that there are two thousand million galaxies like ours, and that the scientists say there are hundreds of thousands of stars or planets in each galaxy, these stars or planets could be our kingdoms. An astronomer told me that there is a planet in one constellation that is a million times larger than the distance between Jupiter and the sun. If this is true, it means that the domain of God has plenty of room for us to rule! This idea of our 'kingdoms' is conjecture on my part, but it is feasible.

It is wonderful that God knows how many stars there are – *Who created all these? He who brings out the **starry** host one by one, and calls them each by name. Because of his great power and mighty strength, not one of them is missing* (Isaiah 40:26). *He determines the number of the **stars** and calls them each by name* (Psalm 147:4). To those who say that the stars and planets are uninhabitable, I would say that, although this is true while we have our present bodies with all their limitations, after our death and resurrection we have new bodies (dealt with in chapter 5 – 'What is Heaven Like?'). These new bodies have no limitations. Where then will be the problem? In any case, God took the original earth which was – *formless and empty, darkness was over the surface of the deep* (Genesis 1:2), and made it into a world which He looked at and said – *it was very good...* (Genesis 1:31). Seeing that God has not changed, He can do it all over again, and again, and again with one star or planet after another ad infinitum! And we will be there with Him!

The question arises 'who will we reign over?' Again, I am not too sure, but the Scriptures indicate that there will be nations at the end times – *To him who overcomes and does my will to the end, I will give authority over the* **nations** (Revelation 2:26). Other Scriptures mention that we will judge, or rule **angels** – *Do you not know that we will* **judge angels?** (1 Corinthians 6:3). There are some things about which I think it best to wait and see – this is one of them!

Will every Christian be a king? Or are there conditions for ruling in God's domain? There is a cautionary note in Scripture – *if we endure, we will also* **reign with him**. *If we disown him, he will also disown us* (2 Timothy 2:12). God does not entrust thrones to those who are afraid of suffering while on earth. Some of my friends believe that the only people to reign as kings are the martyrs mentioned in Revelation – *When he opened the fifth seal, I saw under the altar the souls of those who had been slain because of the word of God and the testimony they had maintained* (Revelation 6:9). I do not believe this but it is right to be a bit selective when we are talking about kings! If God saw that we did not overcome our difficulties and trials on earth, if we do not . . . **reign in life** *through the one man, Jesus Christ* (Romans 5:17), and if we are not – . . . **more than conquerors** *through him who loved us* (Romans 8:37), then God is not likely to entrust us with government in the Kingdom of Heaven! Even Jesus, the King of all kings had to show His Father that He was victorious over trial and temptation on earth, and that He was therefore qualified to reign! It was the path the Master trod, should not His servants tread it still?

The Kingdom of God – stage three

I am still not sure whether the New Earth is the present earth renewed by fire, as in the Bible – *By the same word the present heavens and earth are reserved for fire, being kept for the day of judgment and destruction of ungodly men* (2 Peter

3:7), or whether it will be a brand new earth, though I tend to agree with the quote I gave in chapter 4 – 'Where is Heaven?' – 'It is the same Heaven and earth, but gloriously rejuvenated ... the old order has vanished ... all Creation's potential is now fully realised.'

Old and New

The Bible speaks of the destruction of the 'old' Heaven and Earth – *In the beginning you laid the foundations of the earth, and the heavens are the work of your hands. They will **perish**, but you remain; they will all wear out like a garment. Like clothing you will **change** them and they will be **discarded*** (Psalm 102:25, 26). *I tell you the truth, until heaven and earth **disappear**, not the smallest letter, not the least stroke of a pen, will by any means disappear from the Law until everything is accomplished* (Matthew 5:18). But please bear in mind what I have written in chapter 23 – 'Hell is Eternal' – that 'destruction' and 'perishing' do not mean ceasing to exist, but things in a different form. God's cleansing of Heaven and Earth will be very thorough – *But the day of the Lord will come like a thief. The heavens will disappear with a roar; **the elements will be destroyed by fire**, and the earth and everything in it will be laid bare* (2 Peter 3:10). Every trace of evil, death, damage, and ugliness will disappear. As Peter says in 2 Peter 3:13 it will be *the home of righteousness*. All this is part of the process by which God will bring His eternal plan to fruition. After this wonderful renewal of all things, God can get on with the activities of the new Kingdom. This Kingdom will be absolutely satisfying and fulfilling, both for God and for us.

What about time in Heaven?

Time often seems to be our enemy down here. We have to be in a certain place by a certain time and everything seems to hinder us from doing so. But in Heaven we will be free from such frustration. It is not necessarily true that time will be no more in Heaven. The Bible does not clearly say so. The verse often quoted does not use the word time but delay – *And he swore by him who lives for ever and ever, who created the heavens and all that is in them, the earth and all that is in it, and the sea and all that is in it, and said, 'There will be no more **delay**!'* (Revelation 10:6).

There was a delay for centuries in the unfolding of the 'mystery of God', i.e. His plan of salvation. As the Bible says – *Now to him who is able to establish you by my gospel and the proclamation of Jesus Christ, according to the revelation of the mystery **hidden for long ages past**, but **now** **revealed** and made known through the prophetic writings by the command of the eternal God, so that all nations might believe and obey him* (Romans 16:25, 26).

Now that the Plan had been revealed and accomplished, there was no reason for further delay. But the Bible does not specifically say that there will not be times and seasons of some sort. I cannot be dogmatic as to whether Heaven has a timescale or seasons of activity, but it is possible. The major thing to me is that there will be no pressure, frustration, or deadlines.

A comment worth reading is –

'Paul nowhere affirms that to the life of man, after the close of this aeon, no more duration, no more divisibility in time units shall exist ... The computations of time will be entirely different on the other side of the grave than they are here, where miles and hours are our standard of measurement.'

(Dr G. Vos, quoted by William Hendriksen
in *The Bible and the Hereafter*)

There are many limitations on us here on earth. Disabilities of all sorts afflict us, whether they are physical, mental, or circumstantial. Time is not on our side on occasions. There is so much to do, yet time runs out. I was reminded of this when I read an article by Max Eastman from *The Readers Digest Bedside Book of Discoveries*. In the article he was interviewing Dr Selman Waksman an eminent microbiologist – I quote excerpts from the article here.

Dr Waksman said:

'the living organisms in a thimbleful of average soil outnumber the human population of the United States ... there must be several thousand species of bacteria alone, and there are many differing strains in each species. But besides the bacteria there are the viruses, the protozoa, the fungi, algae, and so on ... a thousand bacteria placed side by side would just reach across the thin edge of a small coin. If you put a thousand million into a cubic centimetre of space, each would have about as much room as a person has in New York City ... it will take hundreds of years to identify and classify all the micro-organisms ... in fact it will never be done, for new strains of each species are constantly arising.'

If such an eminent man can only examine a few of these organisms in his lifetime, and even then not find out everything about them, how can he ever be satisfied when so much is out of his reach. His lifetime is not long enough. But one of the great things about Heaven is that there are no limitations – no shortage of time! Whether there will be microbes in Heaven I don't know, but I do know that there will be plenty of opportunity for research and discovery in that fascinating place.

Heaven is a place of progress

I speak carefully here – but it seems reasonable to suppose that if God is a Creator, and He does not change, presumably He must be creating all the time. Perhaps the Universe gives us a clue; if, as they say, it is constantly expanding, when are we ever to see the end of it? Only those who have eternal life will be able to see it, and even that will take us all our time!

There is nothing static in Heaven because it is a place of activity and wonderful progress. Even on earth Daniel was told that – (in) *the time of the end; many shall run to and fro, and knowledge shall increase* (Daniel 12:4 NKJV). There will be a constant flow of discovery, learning, and understanding. Just consider the progress we have made in the last 50 years on this earth. Things such as TV, penicillin, frozen food, plastic, contact lenses, radar, atomic physics, lasers, ballpoint pens, air-conditioning, drip-dry clothes, voyages to the moon, computers, FM radio, tape recorders, artificial hearts. All this, and we have surely not reached the limit of what God has invented, and man will discover? If there are so many wonderful things being discovered on earth, will there be any less things discovered in the Kingdom of Heaven? Will God ever be outdone by man? It is a pity that so many human discoveries have been used for destructive purposes, but in the Kingdom all discoveries will be beneficial, constructive, and used for the benefit of everyone. Science only means knowledge acquired through discovery. Everything so far produced on earth was already there in essence to discover, so there is no scope for boasting amongst scientists.

Instant knowledge?

I do not believe that we suddenly know everything when we get to Heaven, so that we do not need to learn anymore. It could be boring if we had no incentive to enquire or discover. Even on earth we need some interest or project to satisfy us, and this demands time, for we cannot take in everything at once. God alone knows everything for He is The Deity. Praise Him that He gives us His life, but He does not impart to us His deity so that we also know all things.

If He did, we would be God! It would be boring if there were no further discoveries to be made in the Kingdom. We discover things in stages on earth; we change in stages. As we increase in our likeness to Jesus down here, we do so in stages, it does not happen all at once. It is a process as Scripture says – *And we, who with unveiled faces all reflect the Lord's glory, are being transformed into his likeness with ever-increasing glory, which comes from the Lord, who is the Spirit* (2 Corinthians 3:18). So, perhaps we will only be able to comprehend the glory of Jesus, and the wonder of His Creation in stages. I believe we will need to do so in Heaven even with our new eyes and minds. So, there must be glorious progress up there, both in comprehension, and in activities. I think this will be far more exciting than instant knowledge of everything at once.

Realism

I want to be realistic about these Heavenly truths. It is no good studying the rule of God in the future Kingdom if we are not obeying His rule here on earth. Because Kingdom means rule, we as Christians must show our obedience to His rule while down here. God must be seen in our lives and expressed through our testimony here. Having been joined at the Wedding with Jesus in a wonderful close relationship which will never end, we come into the Kingdom which Jesus taught us to think about and to extend while we are on earth. He meant us to be very keen to advance the rule of God on earth as He made plain in the prayer He taught us to pray – *Thy Kingdom come on earth as it is in Heaven*. He is equally keen for us to extend His rule and realm all through eternity. We are called to such a high destiny – may we live up to the sheer nobility of our calling. Seeing that we are called to such heights, think again about the fact that we are so valuable in God's sight . . .

LINK

Chapter 15

Man's Value in God's Sight

In this chapter I want to link the two sections of this book. I hope that my review of Heaven has shown the great value which God puts on mankind. The glorious destiny He has prepared for us surely shows it. The trouble He has gone to in order to make it possible to enter Heaven shows it. Why then do I write in the next section about Hell? My answer is that God has to show that He hates sin as much as He loves repentant sinners, and that He refuses to have sin in Heaven. He has gone to the utmost lengths to make it possible for mankind to enter Heaven. He spared nothing in order to do it – even when it meant sending His own Son to die for us. He has ordained that Jesus is the only Saviour, and therefore the only way to Heaven. He will bar the door to anyone who refuses to enter by Jesus who said – *I am the gate; whoever enters through me will be saved. He will come in and go out, and find pasture* (John 10:9). For those who refuse His offer of Salvation through Jesus He has prepared a place for them to go when they die. But, because He is so merciful He gives some idea of what it is like so that mankind can be warned, and escape that awful destiny. So it is especially important that we understand Hell as well as Heaven so that we can make the facts known. This is one of the most important tasks of the church. I am aware of the many points of view concerning the doctrine of Hell, but I am trying to concentrate on the major things which we need to understand, and to avoid splitting theological hairs. So let me link the sections on Heaven and that on Hell by writing about –

The value of a soul

At Creation man was good. This was God's opinion – *So God created man in his own image, in the image of God he created him; **male and female** he created them* (Genesis 1:27). *God saw all that he had made, and it was **very good**. And there was evening, and there was morning – the sixth day* (Genesis 1:31). Not only did God regard man as good, He regarded man as valuable. Valuable to Him as a companion; someone for Him to love, and be loved by Him. Valuable as a steward of the earth too. But sin came in through man's pride and disobedience. This did not take God by surprise, but it spoiled the fellowship between God and man. However, it did not lessen his value to God, and He still wanted man to be close to Him. God still . . . *so loved the world that he gave his one and only Son, that whoever believes in him shall not perish but have eternal life* (John 3:16). And He still regarded man as of more value than the whole world. Jesus meant this when He was preaching and said – *What good will it be for a man if he gains the whole world, yet forfeits his soul? Or what can a man give in exchange for his soul?* (Matthew 16:26). So you are of more value than the whole world!

His pursuit of man shows this. Although men evade His Laws, persecute His messengers, and sneer at His Son, God never gives up in His reaching out to mankind. He says in Scripture – *All day long I have held out my hands to an obstinate people, who walk in ways not good, pursuing their own imaginations* (Isaiah 65:2). Even though men and women ignored His messengers, He still sent out more of them – *In the past God spoke to our forefathers through the prophets at many times and in various ways* (Hebrews 1:1). How often has God spoken to you? How many times has He reached out in love in His desire to help you? Why does He do it? For this reason – He loves you; He values you; He wants you.

Think what He did at Calvary. When mankind had rejected His prophets, God did not give up, but He sent His precious Son to say to the world 'I love you, and I want you'. The Bible tells us that – *He who did not spare his own Son, but gave him up for us all – how will he not also, along with him, graciously give us all things?* (Romans 8:32). What more could God do to show His love to us? Jesus was the most precious thing that God could give. Although Jesus never sinned, He was made sin for us. This is something which I have tried to grasp for years but it still eludes me, for it is such a staggering truth. It is the verse – *God made him who had no sin to be sin for us, so that in him we might become the righteousness of God* (2 Corinthians 5:21). He was regarded by God as the sole culprit for the world's sin. We were the sinners; we deserved to die, and yet all our sins were loaded on to Him, as it says – *We all, like sheep, have gone astray, each of us has turned to his own way; and the* LORD *has laid on him the iniquity of us all* (Isaiah 53:6). Why did He do it? Partly to do His Father's will, and because of the value that He sets on us. If that does not impress you, then nothing will. If it does impress you, what response will you make to God?

Does Satan value human beings? Yes, he does, but for very different reasons from God's reasons. To Satan man is only valuable as a means of robbing God of the worship and service which men and women ought to give to Him. Satan wants people to worship him and to allow his princes and demons to control their lives. If he can dominate mankind through drugs, immorality, cruelty and other sins, then he is able to express through them his hatred of God. He has no other way of doing so except through sinning people. What is man's opinion of his own value? Does man value himself at all? Yes, some do, but again his reasons for doing so vary. For example a Christian has a very different system of values to those of a non-Christian.

The average non-Christian does not often think of his or her personal value at all. Those who do, are vague about it. In fact the majority of non-Christians tend to live as the

Bible puts it – *But see, there is joy and revelry, ... 'Let us eat and drink,' you say, 'for tomorrow we die!'* (Isaiah 22:13). The Bible speaks of them in strong terms – *Their destiny is destruction, their god is their stomach, and their glory is in their shame. Their mind is on earthly things* (Philippians 3:19). Other non-Christian people see life on earth only as a means of expressing themselves and fulfilling all their natural desires. Some among them who are power-seekers only see their fellows as a means of helping their own schemes forward.

On the other hand a true Christian has a very different estimate of his value in God's sight. He realises that the new birth has made him a new creature (2 Corinthians 5:17). He is redeemed, changed, and has a new life altogether. A Christian reads the Bible and sees within it how precious he is to God. Look at these examples of God's attitude toward us – *He brought me out into a spacious place; he rescued me because **he delighted in me*** (Psalm 18:19). Another verse says – *The LORD your God is with you, he is mighty to save. He will take great delight in you, he will quiet you with his love, **he will rejoice over you with singing*** (Zephaniah 3:17). Jesus, in His great prayer said to His Father – *let the world know that you sent me and have loved them even as you have loved me* (John 17:23).

A Christian, though aware of his own weaknesses and failures, is equally aware of God's understanding. He will read the Psalm with great joy and relief – *As a father has compassion on his children, so the LORD has compassion on those who fear him* (Psalm 103:13). Stimulated and encouraged by this, he joyfully works with God as his Lord and Father. He will therefore, resist the devil's discouragements and lies about his standing with God. He will also regard his fellow Christians as equally valuable to God. Or, if he doesn't, he ought to!

If, as Christians we have a low opinion of our worth in God's sight, we should remember the insult we offer to Him by rejecting, even unconsciously, His estimate of our value. Doing so is to reject the work of the Holy Spirit as He makes us more like Jesus – *For those God foreknew he also predestined to be conformed to the likeness of his Son, that he might be the firstborn among many brothers* (Romans 8:29).

Remember that the Saviour in us is an Evangelist

Many non-Christians do not think about the eternal future and they are afraid to think of the after-life. Others do think about it, but make the mistake of dabbling in the occult to find something exciting or mysterious. Jesus longs to have them with Him forever, but He has decided to work through us. So how should we view those who do not realise the great value which God sets on them? A Christian should regard a non-Christian with something of the same compassion with which God regards them. We are able to do so because – . . . *we have the* **mind of Christ** (1 Corinthians 2:16). This will cause a Christian to do his utmost to reach out to him with the Gospel, knowing that without it, he is damned forever. He will tell him that there is a Heaven to be gained, and a Hell to be shunned. Ask yourself some questions. Are you selfish with the Gospel? Do you know the whole Gospel? If your answers are 'yes' to the first question, and 'no' to the last, and if you need any help with knowing or preaching the Gospel, be encouraged; faulty understanding can be rectified! It requires effort on our part, and the help of the Holy Spirit. But He is willing if you are! How God's heart rejoices over the prospect of having His precious Children with Him forever. How His heart must grieve over those who have refused their eternal destiny. How God must yearn for us to reach out to them on His behalf. What will you do about His feelings? What will you do with the precious Gospel? If you do not know it well enough, perhaps the last chapter in this book will help you. Try it! Meanwhile we must try to understand the doctrine of Hell in the next chapters. Hell is the only alternative to Heaven.

SECTION 2:

Hell

Chapter 16

Hell is Necessary

The doctrine of Hell is badly neglected today. We are far more ready to preach about love than judgement. But, preaching only about the love of God is akin to heresy: it gives a distorted picture of God. The modern ridiculing of the doctrine of Hell, especially in the media, leads many Christians to avoid the subject, preferring to speak of more pleasant things. This ridicule also helps to increase a sense of false security in unbelievers. It helps them to consign the whole thing to the realms of fantasy. What will they feel when they are separated forever from the only One who can give them eternal security? And what will we feel if, at the Judgement Seat of Christ, we have to admit that we preferred not to offend the unsaved with an unpopular doctrine?

God does nothing which is unnecessary. In the beginning God and man walked happily together because there was no sin to hinder their fellowship. Then sin came in, and everything changed. Sin had to be punished, and that had to take place somewhere. God saw that some men would choose to be apart from Him forever, so He provided a place for them to go. This place was Hell. It was needed, so God provided it. Some people argue that if God was to be tolerant, then Hell would be unnecessary. Tolerance is a much used word today, especially by those who emphasise man's freedom to do what he likes. But God hates this kind

169

of humanistic tolerance. One of the old prophets spoke in a way that rebukes the modern humanists, including some, though not all of the penal reform advocates who are very soft on punishment, and strong on man's rights – *Jehu the seer, the son of Hanani, went out to meet him and said to the king, 'Should you **help the wicked** and **love those who hate the Lord**? Because of this, the wrath of the Lord is upon you'* (2 Chronicles 19:2). God even accuses His church of this wrong tolerance – *Nevertheless, I have this against you: **You tolerate** that woman Jezebel, who calls herself a prophetess. By her teaching she misleads my servants into sexual immorality and the eating of food sacrificed to idols* (Revelation 2:20). On earth we could say 'evil triumphs when people are too tolerant'.

Hell is necessary for several reasons

I will mention them here, and then go into each one in greater detail in the following chapters.

Hell is necessary because of the seriousness of sin

God has only one reaction to sin – hatred and abhorrence of it. How could He refrain from punishing sin? – *How much more severely do you think a man deserves to be punished who has trampled the Son of God under foot, who has treated as an unholy thing the blood of the covenant that sanctified him, and who has insulted the Spirit of grace?* (Hebrews 10:29). God has gone to such great lengths to deal with sin and to provide a way of escape from its consequences so – *how shall we escape if we ignore such a great salvation? This salvation, which was first announced by the Lord, was confirmed to us by those who heard him* (Hebrews 2:3). Contemplating Calvary will help us to see how deeply He hates sin, and how right His attitude is toward it. In the light of His attitude we must learn to hate sin as He does, then we will turn away from it more readily, and we will not preach an easy Gospel.

Hell is needed because God cannot bear to be with sin

Your eyes are too pure to look on evil; you cannot tolerate wrong (Habakkuk 1:13).

How then could He possibly allow unrepentant sinners into His Home? I repeat the Scripture which I have used a number of times in this book – *Nothing impure will ever enter it, nor will anyone who does what is shameful or deceitful, but only those whose names are written in the Lamb's book of life* (Revelation 21:27).

Nor can sinners bear to be with a holy God

God-hating sinners are referred to in the Scripture – *They called to the mountains and the rocks, 'Fall on us and hide us from the face of him who sits on the throne and from the wrath of the Lamb!'* (Revelation 6:16). They hate God, and He hates their sin. How can they live together? Amos put it this way – *Do two walk together unless they have agreed to do so?* (Amos 3:3). Obviously not.

Hell is necessary because of the need of punishment

As I say in chapter 22 – 'God's Punishment of Sin', it is a very unpopular concept today. Much, though not all of today's psychology teaches that we must allow children to do what they want to do, without restraint. They say that we can inhibit a child's development if we are restrictive. This is not the teaching of Scripture. God believes in punishment for sin. However, His punishment always fits the crime, because He is wholly fair and just.

Hell is necessary for the fulfilment of judgement

God takes a careful look at man's record before He pronounces a verdict on it. He misses nothing, and forgets nothing. He then pronounces judgement, which, for the lost is always a condemnation.

Hell is needed because there must be a choice

Choice for man

God gave us free will, and He honours it. Some chose not to

receive Him as Lord – *He came to that which was his own, but his own did not receive him* (John 1:11). Others did accept Him as Lord and Father – *Yet to all who received him, to those who believed in his name, he gave the right to become children of God* (John 1:12).

Choice for God

He chose to refuse entry to Heaven for all those who refused to repent and obey Jesus – *Not everyone who says to me, 'Lord, Lord,' will enter the kingdom of heaven, but only he who does the will of my Father who is in heaven* (Matthew 7:21). And He chose to allow the ungodly to go to their chosen destiny – *But the cowardly, the unbelieving, the vile, the murderers, the sexually immoral, those who practise magic arts, the idolaters and all liars – their place will be in the fiery lake of burning sulphur. This is the second death* (Revelation 21:8).

But He gladly chose to receive those who believed on His Son – *Whoever believes in the Son has eternal life...* (John 3:36). God does not delight in providing Hell for those who choose to go there. But He would not be righteous if He did not give man the choice. By the way, He does not throw man into Hell. The Scripture which seems to say that He does needs to be understood – *But I will show you whom you should fear: Fear him who, after the killing of the body, has power to throw you into hell. Yes, I tell you, fear him* (Luke 12:5). We must understand that God does not throw people into Hell **against their will**. He only does it when they have made their decision. He simply confirms the decision which every man makes before he dies.

We must now find out more about this dreadful place. Please do not ignore this section of the book. It is far more pleasant to read the section on Heaven, but are we more concerned about pleasant things for us than we are about the dreadful prospect for some of our close friends and relatives?

Chapter 17

Where is Hell?

First let us define the terms used

Sheol/Hades

Hell is not really the correct word, but it is used in the KJV version of the Bible 54 times to represent the words 'Sheol' or 'Hades'. For example – *For thou wilt not leave my soul in **hell**; neither wilt thou suffer thine Holy One to see corruption* (Psalm 16:10 KJV). *In **hell**, where he was in torment, he looked up and saw Abraham far away, with Lazarus by his side (Luke 16:23). The Bible teaches that there is a temporary Hell and a final Hell.

Opinions vary as to whether the temporary Hell/Sheol/ Hades is one place with two compartments (one for the saved, and the other for the lost), or one place which is only for the spirits of the wicked. It is certain that the spirits of the wicked are somewhere in a temporary place, and will be transferred to somewhere permanent. Hades seems to be the place. It is a temporary prison for them until they are raised from the dead (the second death or resurrection) for their final judgement. Incidentally if it is true that Hades is a place for those awaiting punishment, Christians cannot even be adjacent to it, because Jesus has born our punishment for us, and we are not awaiting it.

Purgatory

Roman Catholics believe in a temporary state for the dead

173

which they call 'Purgatory'. They define it as a place where the departed spirits of saved Roman Catholics are cleansed through suffering. They say that the suffering there is a joyful suffering because they know that the occupants are saved. According to their doctrine, it is not a second chance of salvation, but an experience of cleansing before the final Heaven. A Scripture sometimes quoted in support of this idea is – *If it is burned up, he will suffer loss; he himself will be saved, but only as one escaping through the flames* (1 Corinthians 3:15). But this verse describes the testing of our **works** on the earth, **not** the testing of our **souls**. It talks of our being saved **so as** by fire, not **through** fire. Purgatory is a man-made doctrine having no support at all in Scripture.

Paradise

Some say that this is another name for Hades, or another section in it, but I deal with this more fully in chapter 7 – 'Death'.

So, where are the unsaved dead?

The unsaved are separated from God

Whether in the temporary Hell or the final Hell the ungodly are separated from God. Just as the unsaved are separated from Him in spirit while alive on the earth – *Once you were alienated from God and were enemies in your minds because of your evil behaviour* (Colossians 1:21) – so they will be separated in spirit and in body in Hell. This is illustrated by what Jesus quoted in Scripture – *And besides all this, between us and you **a great chasm has been fixed**, so that those who want to go from here to you cannot, nor can anyone cross over from there to us* (Luke 16:26). In this passage the unsaved rich man is seen in Hell/Hades, already in torment, and separated by an impassable gulf from Paradise. Hell/Hades is a prison for those destined for punishment from which there is no escape.

They are in the temporary Hell

I write more in a later chapter about the final Hell (see chapter 23 – 'Hell is Eternal'). Here I refer to the place where the unsaved go to when they die during the period before the Resurrection.

The final Hell is uninhabited at the moment

Scripture indicates that the **final** Hell is as yet uninhabited, for at the moment, Satan and his demons are in and around the earth. Scripture illustrates this: *The LORD said to Satan, 'Where have you come from?' Satan answered the LORD, 'From roaming through the earth and going to and fro in it'* (Job 1:7); *in which you used to live when you followed the ways of this world and of the ruler of the kingdom of the air, the spirit who is now at work in those who are disobedient* (Ephesians 2:2); *For our struggle is not against flesh and blood, but against the rulers, against the authorities, against the powers of this dark world and against the spiritual forces of evil in* **the Heavenly realms** (Ephesians 6:12). The only exception seems to be some at least of the fallen angels: *For if God did not spare angels when they sinned, but sent them to hell, putting them into gloomy dungeons to be held for judgment* (2 Peter 2:4); *And the angels who did not keep their positions of authority but abandoned their own home – these he has kept in darkness, bound with everlasting chains for judgment on the great Day* (Jude 1:6).

The permanent state of the lost

The final Hell is the abode of the unsaved forever after the judgement of the Great White Throne. This final Hell is called by different names.

- **The Pit** (Revelation 9:1); **The Abyss** (Revelation 20:1; **Lake of fire** (Revelation 20:10); **Gehenna** (Matthew 5:29). All these refer to the same place, using different symbolism – the final abode of the devil, fallen angels, Beast, False Prophet, and all the unsaved.

- **Tartarus** is referred to only once (2 Peter 2:4), and it seems to be the temporary prison for the fallen angels, until they too enter the final Hell.

All these terms refer to the final abode of the devil, fallen angels, Beast, False Prophet, and all the unsaved. There is no escape from this prison; it is guarded by great angels – *And I saw an angel coming down out of Heaven, having the key to the Abyss and holding in his hand a great chain* (Revelation 20:1).

The permanent state of the saved

In the New Heaven. We live there with God forever. More about this in Section 1: Heaven.

Jesus went to Hell

The are two occasions on which Jesus went to Hell. The first was when He went there as part of the punishment for sin on Calvary. After all He must have paid the full penalty for sin, otherwise Calvary would be incomplete.

The second occasion was when Jesus visited Hades again **after** His resurrection. He went and – ... *preached to the spirits in prison who disobeyed long ago when God waited patiently in the days of Noah while the ark was being built. In it only a few people, eight in all, were saved through water* (1 Peter 3:19–20). He did not go to Hades to preach the Gospel, because those imprisoned there are beyond redemption. Instead He proclaimed His triumph in front of them as He rose from the dead. In support of my view I quote from Derek Prince who says in his *Foundation Series* Vol. 3, p. 69 –

> 'The Greek verb here translated 'preached' is directly connected with the Greek noun 'herald'. It does not therefore necessarily indicate that Christ 'preached the Gospel' to the spirits in prison; but merely that He made to them some 'proclamation', such as a herald would make.'

Jesus did not stay in Hell

God the Father would not allow it. The one offering for sin forever was accepted. God raised Him from the dead, and that was that – ... *he spoke of the resurrection of the Christ, that he was not abandoned to the grave, nor did his body see decay* (Acts 2:31). He returned in triumph to His Father. Then, if the scholars are right, He must have brought the believing dead out of the 'good' compartment of Hades, taking them with Him to Heaven.

After His resurrection Jesus showed Himself alive to many people, thus demonstrating His triumph on earth as well as in Hades: *After that, he appeared to more than five hundred of the brothers at the same time, most of whom are still living, though some have fallen asleep* (1 Corinthians 15:6); *After his suffering, he showed himself to these men and gave many convincing proofs that he was alive. He appeared to them over a period of forty days and spoke about the kingdom of God* (Acts 1:3). I wonder if Jesus spoke to them about His experiences in Hades?

The next chapter is one of the hardest things I have ever written. To describe Hell is like being there for a split second.

Chapter 18

What is Hell Like?

It may be wise to pray for special grace from God before you read this section. I could not write it without weeping. I hope you will not read it without weeping. It is too terrible for words, and yet we must find some way of contemplating its horrors in case we become insensitive to the needs of those, including some of our loved ones, who are heading for Hell. I have not written very fully about it, in case I seem to gloat over such punishment, but I write at some length so that we can see how terrible Hell is.

Who are the inhabitants of Hell?

The inhabitants also include the Beast and False Prophet – *And the devil, who deceived them, was thrown into the lake of burning sulphur, where the beast and the false prophet had been thrown. They will be tormented day and night for ever and ever* (Revelation 20:10). Who would want to live in such a place with such evil beings at close range! As if Hell is not bad enough with the devil and the others in it, there are more evil beings there too. They are the fallen angels who God imprisoned in darkness beforehand – *For if God did not spare angels when they sinned, but sent them to Hell, putting them into gloomy dungeons to be held for judgment* (2 Peter 2:4). *And the angels who did not keep their positions of authority but abandoned their own home – these he has kept in darkness, bound with everlasting chains for judgment on the great Day* (Jude 1:6). The company in Hell includes all those whose names are not written in the Book of Life – *If anyone's name was not found written in the book of life, he was thrown into the lake of fire* (Revelation 20:15).

What is it like?

The ethos, or atmosphere of a place is set by its inhabitants. People make places. After many years in the North of England I went back to visit Harrow where I grew up. As a boy I knew most of the neighbours, and played with many of the children. It was familiar, because I knew the place. But when I returned, it seemed like a different place. It was the people whom I knew who had made it what is was to me, but now they were gone, the atmosphere was not the same. In Hell the atmosphere is determined by its chief inhabitant, Satan, who is a liar and murderer, among other things. He is evil personified, therefore the ethos of his prison can only be unlimited evil continually.

It is a prison

There is no longer any access to the God who could have changed them in their life on earth. As I said in chapter 17 – 'Where is Hell?', they are separated from God – and here I say they are in a prison. I use the same Scripture to prove this similar point – *And besides all this, **between us and you there is a great gulf fixed**, so that those who want to pass from here to you cannot, nor can those from there pass to us* (Luke 16:26 NKJV). Having used this passage several times to illustrate different points I want to say that this account in the Bible is not a parable, or an illustration, it is a statement of truth. Jesus plainly said *There was a certain rich man....* The passage indicates that existence in Hades, and the final Hell is somewhat like life here and now in its worst aspects. It also proves that those in these awful places are conscious, thinking, talking, remembering, fearful, tormented. The rich man was – *In Hell, where he was in torment, he looked* *up and saw Abraham far away, with Lazarus by his side. So he called to him, 'Father Abraham, have pity on me and send Lazarus to dip the tip of his finger in water and cool my tongue, because I am in agony in this fire'* (Luke 16:23–24). The ungodly are capable of sensation; they are not unconscious or impervious to it. The rich man speaks about his tongue, and he must either have eyes, or some ability to see because he sees Abraham. I believe that they will have bodies at the resurrection and in the final Hell. I realise that the following verse may be figurative and not literal but I quote it as a **possible** illustration of the body in the after-life – *If your hand causes you to sin, cut it off. It is better for you to enter life maimed than with two **hands** to go into Hell, where the fire never goes out* (Mark 9:43). If my theory is right, their bodies are not like the new bodies of the saved, but like their old ones, lacking in ability to be satisfied.

It is a foul place

Death does not alter character. Those in Hell refused God's new life, either deliberately, or by neglect, therefore they are set in the mould of their old life. Think if you dare about the foul character of those in Hell. God describes them in the Bible – *But the cowardly, the unbelieving, the vile, the murderers, the sexually immoral, those who practise magic arts, the idolaters and all liars – their place will be in the fiery lake of burning sulphur. This is the second death* (Revelation 21:8). They will never change for God's edict is that their state will be fixed – **forever**. *Let him who does wrong continue to do wrong; let him who is vile continue to be vile; let him who does right continue to do right; and let him who is holy continue to be holy* (Revelation 22:11). Therefore, Hell will be continually full of people who can never do anything good, kind, loving, or beautiful – just like their overlord Satan. Demons will be there too; they operated on earth, and they will be in Hell. Their character will not change, so they will be tormenting in Hell as they did on earth. *A Canaanite woman from that vicinity came to him,* crying out, *'Lord, Son of David, have mercy on me! My daughter is **suffering terribly from demon-possession'*** (Matthew 15:22). Demons do not change, so they will torment those in Hell as they did on earth.

It is a place of suffering

The ungodly suffer on earth in a similar way to that awaiting them in eternity. Consider the sufferings of the people on earth mentioned in the Bible – *Some sat in darkness and the deepest gloom, prisoners **suffering in iron chains*** (Psalm 107:10). They suffered because – *they had rebelled against the words of God and despised the counsel of the Most High* (Psalm 107:11). Because of these sins they suffered the consequences. The Bible says elsewhere – *You will **suffer the penalty** for your lewdness and bear the consequences of your sins of idolatry. Then you will know that I am the Sovereign* LORD (Ezekiel 23:49). Their sufferings on earth were a foretaste of those awaiting them in Hell. Man's disobedience on earth will cause them to suffer in Hell forever. There is a certain justice in that some places such as Sodom and Gommorrah in which the people give themselves over to sin while alive on the earth should suffer the consequences in Hell. They **chose** to sin as the Bible says – *In a similar way, Sodom and Gomorrah and the surrounding towns **gave themselves up** to sexual immorality and perversion. They serve as an example of those who **suffer the punishment of eternal fire*** (Jude 1:7). Their sin caused great hurt to the righteous people around them, now it is their turn to suffer. It is nobody's fault but their own.

As our substitute Jesus suffered the pangs of death and Hell at Calvary – *But we see Jesus, who was made a little lower than the angels, now crowned with glory and honour because he suffered death, so that by the grace of God he might taste death for everyone* (Hebrews 2:9). *After the suffering of his soul, he will see the light of life and be satisfied; by his knowledge my righteous servant will justify many, and he will bear their iniquities* (Isaiah 53:11). I have enlarged a little on this in chapter 20 – 'The Judgement Day'.

Absence of joy

The deepest sorrow experienced on earth pales into insignificance beside the sorrows of Hell. There is no joy there. The Bible declares that joy comes through being near to God – *you will fill me with **joy in your presence**, with eternal pleasures at your right hand* (Psalm 16:11). Those in Hell are far away from God; how then can they ever be joyful?

Weeping

The absence of joy brings sorrow, and this usually leads to weeping. On earth weeping can be a relief, and a release of tension – ... *weeping may remain for a night, but rejoicing comes in the morning* (Psalm 30:5), but in Hell weeping is continuous and brings no relief because there is no hope there – *But the subjects of the kingdom will be thrown outside, into the darkness, where there will be weeping and gnashing of teeth* (Matthew 8:12).

Frustration

There will be a terrible inability to express anything, because there is no possibility of being creative. Satan is not creative – only God is, together with the people who have His nature. Because the devil cannot create, those incarcerated with him will have his uncreative nature. So there will be no means of satisfaction or fulfilment, because nothing will be tangible or attainable.

Restlessness

God describes the atmosphere in Hell through John the Apostle – *And the smoke of their torment rises for ever and ever. There is **no rest day or night** for those who worship the beast and his image, or for anyone who receives the mark of his name* (Revelation 14:11). The solemn verdict given by God on those who reject Him is that – *They shall **never enter** my rest* (Hebrews 3:11). Sadly – *'There is no peace,' says the* LORD, *'for the wicked'* (Isaiah 48:22). Oh that men and women would accept the Lordship of Christ and thereby enter His rest now, while it is possible.

Fire

The Bible speaks of fire in Hell – *But I tell you that anyone who is angry with his brother will be subject to judgment. Again, anyone who says to his brother, 'Raca,' is answerable to the Sanhedrin. But anyone who says, 'You fool!' will be in danger of the fire of Hell* (Matthew 5:22). *Then he will say to those on his left, 'Depart from me, you who are cursed, into the eternal fire prepared for the devil and his angels* (Matthew 25:41). There may be actual flames in this fire in Hell, or they may be metaphorical. For example, the 'flames' of remorse, 'If only' is a powerful pang. The 'flames' of lost opportunity will torment them forever. Regret could be another 'flame'. And a longing for things which are unattainable in the Abyss could be a 'flame'. Whether these flames are actual or metaphorical, the fact is that they are a terrible aspect of this awful place.

Wrath

The occupants of Hell are continually aware of God's wrath. It is the fulfilment of the verse – *Whoever believes in the Son has eternal life, but whoever rejects the Son will not see life, for God's wrath remains on him* (John 3:36).

I have written in more detail about wrath in chapter 21 – 'The Anger of God'.

Punishment

I have written more about punishment in chapter 22 – 'God's Punishment of Sin'.

No mercy

God will not have mercy on any of the inhabitants of Hell. In any case, it will not be possible to find Him. It is not that He sits in malicious pleasure over the state of the lost. He went to the utmost lengths to deliver them from His anger in their lifetime, and He stretched out His hands every day to a rebellious people, offering them mercy. *All day long I have held out my hands to an obstinate people, who walk in ways not good, pursuing their own imaginations* (Isaiah 65:2). If men decided to flout His Laws after the many warnings He gave them, they paid the penalty – *Anyone who rejected the law of Moses died without mercy on the testimony of two or three witnesses* (Hebrews 10:28). It is easy to think of what happened to people centuries ago and to say that such things are not for today. But Jesus, the Author of the New Covenant plainly warned the disciples – *Do not think that I have come to abolish the Law or the Prophets; I have not come to abolish them but to fulfil them* (Matthew 5:17). But there will still be those who will argue that His Law was only for the early disciples but not for us in our generation. But God says – *I the LORD do not change...* (Malachi 3:6). If He does not change, neither do His Laws, except perhaps the dietary instructions.

Torment

The Greek word for 'torment' means 'going to the very bottom'; 'torture'; 'retribution'. All these will be experienced in Hell. *In Hell, where he was in torment, he looked up and saw Abraham far away, with Lazarus by his side* (Luke 16:23). It is important to realise that it is not God who torments mankind in Hell. People there are tormented by their own minds and memories, and in addition by the enemy himself, with his fallen angels. Those in Hell sink lower and lower in their degradation. They do indeed reach the depths – tormented. Nothing exalts them, because nothing there is noble or uplifting. More than anyone else in Hell Satan will be tormented because he, as the instigator of sin will suffer the consequences – *And the devil, who deceived them, was thrown into the lake of burning sulphur, where the beast and the false prophet had been thrown. They will be tormented day and night for ever and ever* (Revelation 20:10).

Darkness

This darkness is both actual darkness, for God is not there

in His light, and mental and emotional darkness. God does not enjoy allowing people to enter this darkness, but if He withdraws Himself from them it is bound to be dark. When God withdrew from His beloved Son Jesus when He died, the Bible says that – *At the sixth hour darkness came over the whole land until the ninth hour* (Mark 15:33). Jesus was *made sin for us* therefore He became utterly repugnant to God, and the Father had to turn away from Him. Obviously then God turns away from those who choose to go to Hell, and it is indeed dark. Neither men nor angels escape the darkness of Hell – *Then the king told the attendants, 'Tie him hand and foot, and throw him outside, into the darkness, where there will be weeping and gnashing of teeth' (Matthew 22:13). For if God did not spare angels when they sinned, but sent them to Hell, putting them into gloomy dungeons to be held for judgment* (2 Peter 2:4). This darkness has no end – *They are wild waves of the sea, foaming up their shame; wandering stars, for whom **blackest darkness** has been reserved **forever*** (Jude 1:13).

Shame

*Multitudes who sleep in the dust of the earth will awake: some to everlasting life, others to **shame** and everlasting contempt* (Daniel 12:2). I am not sure that they will feel shame, for they may be incapable of it in Hell, but they are in a state of shame, with nothing to uplift them or ennoble them.

Is God in Hell?

This is a difficult question to answer, and I am hesitant to give an answer. But one thing I know is that God is omnipresent. He is everywhere at once. Therefore there cannot be a place anywhere in Creation where He is not present, or shall we say that there is no place where He cannot go **if He wishes to**. David says in the Psalms – *Where can I go from your Spirit? Where can I flee from your presence? If I go up to the heavens, you are there; if I make my bed in the depths, you are there. If I rise on the wings of the dawn, if I settle on the* *far side of the sea, even there your hand will guide me, your right hand will hold me fast. If I say, 'Surely the darkness will hide me and the light become night around me,' even the darkness will not be dark to you; the night will shine like the day, for darkness is as light to you* (Psalm 139:7–12).

'God-forsaken' is a non-term. It is meaningless, except for a while at Calvary where God forsook His Son for a brief time – *And at the ninth hour Jesus cried out in a loud voice, ... 'My God, my God, why have you forsaken me?'* (Mark 15:34). This total separation from God was the real pain of Calvary, where Jesus experienced it until God raised Him up again.

Separation

I believe that God is in charge of all things, even Hell, although He is only 'present' there momentarily in His anger. Scripture seems to indicate that God can visit Hell for specific judgemental purposes on occasions – *he will be tormented with burning sulphur **in the presence of the holy angels and of the Lamb*** (Revelation 14:10). However, God is not there in His love and mercy, but in His anger and righteous judgement.

Separation from the goodness, love, mercy and grace of God will be Hell's greatest torment. God is light, love, joy, mercy, peace, satisfaction, grace, beauty, etc. Imagine being deprived of such things, **forever**. As I have said in chapter 21 –'The Anger of God', God is silent to those in Hell forever.

Before unsaved people go to Hell, they die! So, having dealt with death for the Christian in the section on Heaven, we must now look at death for the unsaved – in the next chapter.

Chapter 19

Death and Resurrection for the Lost

Most people will die before the Resurrection, whether they are saved or lost. They will have made their decision as to where they are going. Death need hold no fears for the Christian, but –

Death is awful for the lost

It is not the process of death so much as the consequences of it which is so awful, as the Bible makes clear: *It is a dreadful thing to fall into the hands of the living God* (Hebrews 10:31); *Just as man is destined to die once, and after that to face judgment* (Hebrews 9:27). There is no hope or blessing for the lost after death – *but only a fearful expectation of judgment and of raging fire that will consume the enemies of God. Anyone who rejected the law of Moses died without mercy on the testimony of two or three witnesses* (Hebrews 10:27–28). It is not just the process of separation of the spirit and the body, but the separation of the spirit from God which is so terrible.

Just as angels gather the saved safely into Heaven, so they gather the lost into Hell. They enforce the decree of Jesus as Scripture indicates – *The Son of Man will send out his angels, and they will weed out of his kingdom everything that causes sin and all who do evil. They will throw them into the fiery furnace, where there will be weeping and gnashing of teeth* (Matthew 13:41–42). They will do the same to the devil himself – *And I saw an angel coming down out of Heaven, having the key to the Abyss and holding in his hand a great chain. He seized the dragon, that ancient serpent, who is the devil, or Satan, and bound him for a thousand years* (Revelation 20:1–2).

After death comes resurrection

Death is the end of one era of our existence, and the beginning of another. All the bodies of all who have ever lived will be raised from either the earth, or the sea, and be reunited with their spirit from wherever they are: either from the Presence of the Lord, or from the place or state where the ungodly are – ... *there will be a resurrection of both the righteous and the wicked* (Acts 24:15).

As I said in chapter 8 – 'There will be a Resurrection', no one can escape resurrection. The Bible says so – *And I saw the dead, great and small, standing before the throne, and books were opened. Another book was opened, which is the book of life. The dead were judged according to what they had done as recorded in the books. The sea gave up the dead that were in it, and death and Hades gave up the dead that were in them, and each person was judged according to what he had done* (Revelation 20:12, 13). These verses refer to the second aspect of the resurrection which is for those who are lost.

As I have said, there may be two resurrections, or there may be one, but with two aspects. Either way, all are resurrected. The King James Version emphasises two aspects of it – *And shall come forth; they that have done good, unto the* **resurrection** *of life; and they that have done evil, unto the* **resurrection** *of damnation* (John 5:29 KJV). *(The rest of the dead did not come to life until the thousand years were ended.) This is the first resurrection.* (Revelation 20:5).

The lost are raised to damnation

This old word in the KJV version of Scripture is better rendered 'condemnation'. The word describes the effect of a judgement given. The state of the one condemned – *If anyone's name was not found written in the book of life, he was thrown into the lake of fire* (Revelation 20:15); *those who have **done evil will rise to be condemned*** (John 5:29). It is the second death. I am not concerned to argue as to whether there are one or two resurrections, but about the terror of the **second death**. This is a description of damnation. *Blessed and holy are those who have part in the first resurrection. **The second death** has no power over them, but they will be priests of God and of Christ and will reign with him for a thousand years* (Revelation 20:6). *But the cowardly, the unbelieving, the vile, the murderers, the sexually immoral, those who practise magic arts, the idolaters and all liars – their place will be in the fiery lake of burning sulphur. **This is the second death*** (Revelation 21:8). This verse needs a little explanation. I do not believe that someone who is cowardly on some occasions is consigned to Hell. But if someone lives in the sins mentioned here continually, and defiantly, and does not repent, then this Scripture becomes relevant. (I deal with these aspects in chapter 20 – 'The Judgement Day'.)

The second death is final

The process of damnation or condemnation is first, rejection of Jesus, then physical death, then resurrection, and judgement, leading to that final state described in the Bible as ... *the lake of fire. The lake of fire is the **second death**. If anyone's name was not found written in the book of life, he was thrown into the lake of fire* (Revelation 20:14–15). This is the final abode, and the final state of the lost.

It is about the Judgement that we now have to write ...

Chapter 20

The Judgement Day

Judgement includes vengeance, avenging, and justice

- 'Justice' means what is right or the execution of what is right.
- 'Judgement' means a decision/verdict based on all the evidence.
- 'Vengeance' means that which proceeds out of justice.
- 'Vengeance' and 'avenging' (Greek: *'ekdikesis'*: vindication; retribution; repayment) – God's vengeance, unlike man's, is free from vindictiveness.

None of these words contradict each other. In Scripture the words are often combined. The NIV blurs the distinction, so I quote from the KJV: *But, O LORD Almighty, you who judge righteously and test the heart and mind, let me see your **vengeance** upon them, for to you I have committed my cause* (Jeremiah 11:20); *For we know him who said, 'It is mine to **avenge**; I will repay,' and again, 'The Lord will judge his people'* (Hebrews 10:30).

Judgement will be meted out in the last Day. There will be a great Court held in the Heavens, or perhaps on the earth. Everyone who has ever been born or created will be there. The occasion is the Resurrection and the Day of judgement – *Multitudes who sleep in the dust of the earth will awake: some to everlasting life, others to shame and*

190

everlasting contempt (Daniel 12:2). For the purposes of this section concerning Hell, the Judgement at the Great White Throne mentioned in Revelation 20:11, is the outstanding thing in this Court, together with the One who sits upon it. Nearly all the Prophets refer to this Day. Some of them like Joel and Amos major on it. The term 'Day' can refer to a time, day, year, or any period of time. The extent of it is not important, the certainty of it happening is the point I am making. It is quite likely that The Second Coming, the Resurrection, and the Judgement Day all happen together. Again, the chronology of these happenings is not important to me. In fact the various theories as to the chronology of these events have provoked too much argument, and there has been more heat than light coming from them!

One Day of Judgement, or several?

I posed a similar question in chapter 8 – 'There will be a Resurrection', as to one resurrection or two, and I reach a similar conclusion in this chapter – that there is one Judgement Day, but with several different aspects to it. Scripture seems to indicate one day: *For he has set **a day** when he will judge the world with justice by the man he has appointed. He has given proof of this to all men by raising him from the dead* (Acts 17:31); *By the same word the present Heavens and earth are reserved for fire, being kept for **the day** of judgement and destruction of ungodly men* (2 Peter 3:7).

But there are several aspects of this Day. They include the judgement of the wicked, the judgement of the nations, and rewards for the righteous. The saved are in focus during one aspect of Judgement (see chapter 11 – 'The Judgement Seat of Christ'); and the unsaved are in focus during the aspect I am dealing with here. The following Scripture seems to include both these aspects – *The nations were angry; and your wrath has come. The time has come for **judging** the dead, and for **rewarding** your servants the prophets and your saints and those who reverence your name,* *both small and great – and for destroying those who destroy the earth* (Revelation 11:18).

The judgement of Christians

The Throne of God is the place where Christians are judged and rewarded. Paul seems to be primarily speaking to Christians when he says – *For we must all appear before the judgement seat of Christ, that each one may receive what is due to him for the things done while in the body, whether good or bad* (2 Corinthians 5:10).

(More about this aspect of Judgement in chapter 11 – 'The Judgement Seat of Christ'.)

The judgement of the nations

Nations change their names from time to time: e.g. Rhodesia is now called Zimbabwe; Persia is now called Iran. But whatever nations may call themselves at the end time, they will stand before God on the great Day – *When the Son of Man comes in his glory, and all the angels with him, he will sit on his throne in Heavenly glory. All the **nations** will be gathered before him, and he will separate the people one from another as a shepherd separates the sheep from the goats. He will put the sheep on his right and the goats on his left. Then the King will say to those on his right, 'Come, you who are blessed by my Father; take your inheritance, the kingdom prepared for you since the creation of the world'* (Matthew 25:31–34).

The judgement of Satan

At last the evil one who has spoiled God's wonderful world, and enslaved so many people in it will be condemned and punished – *And the devil, who deceived them, was thrown into the lake of burning sulphur, where the beast and the false prophet had been thrown. They will be tormented day and night for ever and ever* (Revelation 20:10).

The judgement of fallen angels

The Bible records a strange event – war in Heaven! Satan and some of the angels revolted against God, but they were unable to defeat God, so He threw them out of Heaven, to be judged on the great Day. In fact some of them were imprisoned straightaway – *For if God did not spare angels when they sinned, but sent them to Hell, putting them into gloomy dungeons to be held for judgment* (2 Peter 2:4); *And the angels who did not keep their positions of authority but abandoned their own home – these he has kept in darkness, bound with everlasting chains for judgment on the great Day* (Jude 1:6).

No one escapes this Judgement Day

Just as no one escapes death or resurrection, so, no one escapes the Judgement day when God enforces the separation between the saved and the unsaved – *All the nations will be gathered before him, and he will separate the people one from another as a shepherd separates the sheep from the goats* (Matthew 25:32). There will be no hiding place to escape to. The Bible is very accurate about this – . . . *For we will all stand before God's judgment seat* (Romans 14:10); *So then, **each of us** will give an account of himself to God* (Romans 14:12). How can anyone evade God? The Psalmist points out the impossibility of doing so – *Where can I go from your Spirit? Where can I flee from your presence?* (Psalm 139:7); *If I go up to the Heavens, you are there; if I make my bed in the depths, you are there* (Psalm 139:8). Judgement will be meted out to everyone, although the judgement of Christians will not include damnation.

Some will try to escape from it

They called to the mountains and the rocks, 'Fall on us and hide us from the face of him who sits on the throne and from the wrath of the Lamb!' (Revelation 6:16). *During those days men will seek death, but will not find it; they will long to die, but death will elude them* (Revelation 9:6). The terrible thing about this Judgement Day for those who are lost is the fact that there is no escape from it. It is impossible to avoid standing before the Almighty.

No one can prevent this Day from happening

God the Almighty has ordained it. Let the cynics who dispute the fact of Judgement hear the Word of God: *For he has set a day when he will judge the world with justice by the man he has appointed. He has given proof of this to all men by raising him from the dead* (Acts 17:31); *God is not a man, that he should lie, nor a son of man, that he should change his mind. Does he speak and then not act? Does he promise and not fulfil?* (Numbers 23:19). God does seem to be slow to fulfil His Word, but He never fails to do so.

The reason for this Day

Perfect Judgement must be done, and it must be seen to have been done. God is very patient with this sinful world, but that does not mean that He shuts His eyes to its iniquity. Nor does He approve of it. There is only one attitude which He can have to it, and that is one of judgement. The problem comes with modern use of this word. It is used as something which is cruel, unfeeling, and intolerant. God's judgement is not like that.

God's judgement is intended to restrain evil

And the Lord said, Behold, the people is one, and they have all one language; and this they begin to do: and now nothing will be restrained from them, which they have imagined to do (Genesis 11:6 KJV). If God had not flooded the earth, mankind would have gone on to unimaginable evil because they had thrown off all restraint. Similarly, in the end times, Satan (the lawless one) will make every effort to make mankind throw off all restraint again. He is mentioned in Scripture in this context – *Don't let anyone deceive you in any way, for that day will not come until the rebellion occurs and the man of lawlessness is revealed, the man doomed to destruction* (2 Thessalonians 2:3). Thank God for the Holy Spirit who holds him back, as in the verse – *And now you know what is holding him back, so that he may be revealed at the proper time* (2 Thessalonians 2:6). My understanding of *what is holding him back* is the Holy Spirit's restraint. Consider the tragedy in the High Priest Eli's family – *For I told him that I would judge his family forever because of the sin he knew about; his sons made themselves contemptible, and he failed to restrain them* (1 Samuel 3:13). Eli's restraining could have preserved his son's lives. It could be true of many families today. If God is loving enough to severely restrain people in order to avert tragedy in the world, let us be severe if necessary in order to avert tragedy in our families.

His judgement is entirely justified

The Judgement of God is righteous, as Scripture shows – *But because of your stubbornness and your unrepentant heart, you are storing up wrath against yourself for the day of God's wrath, when his **righteous judgment** will be revealed* (Romans 2:5). Righteous judgement is impartial judgement. It is entirely free from malice, even though man continually broke His Laws. He offered mankind abundant life, and all the help they needed – *... I have come that they may have life, and have it to the full* (John 10:10). But tragically He had to say to so many – *yet you refuse to come to me to have life* (John 5:40). His Laws were given, not to be a burden, but to be a safeguard and a blessing. God kept warning men to be careful. *In the past God spoke to our forefathers through the prophets at many times and in various ways, but in these last days he has spoken to us by his Son, whom he appointed heir of all things, and through whom he made the universe* (Hebrews 1:1–2).

God even judged His Son

God is so concerned for proper judgement that He even judged His own Son. Jesus was made the sole culprit for the world's sin instead of us – *For Christ died for sins once for all, the righteous for the unrighteous, to bring you to God. He was put to death in the body but made alive by the Spirit* (1 Peter 3:18). *God made him who had no sin to be sin for us, so that in him we might become the righteousness of God* (2 Corinthians 5:21). This complete judgement of Jesus by the Father involved that total separation which is the major aspect of the terror of Hell. Consider – *And at the ninth hour Jesus cried out in a loud voice, 'Eloi, Eloi, lama sabachthani?' – which means, 'My God, my God, why have you forsaken me?'* (Mark 15:34). Why did God forsake His Son? So that He would not have to forsake you!

The Judge

This Judge is Jesus

The same Jesus who was judged for our sin is now the Judge of those who rejected the salvation which He had just accomplished for mankind – *Moreover, the Father judges no-one, but has entrusted all judgment to the Son* (John 5:22). *This will take place on the day when God will judge men's secrets through Jesus Christ, as my gospel declares* (Romans 2:16).

The character of a judge is all important. The Bible describes the character of Jesus, the righteous Judge – *Righteousness will be his belt and faithfulness the sash round his waist* (Isaiah 11:5). In fact, no one could find any fault in the character of Jesus – *Can any of you prove me guilty of sin? If I am telling the truth, why don't you believe me?* (John 8:46).

The judgement the judge metes out must be righteous judgement too. Again, Jesus is not found wanting – *But because of your stubbornness and your unrepentant heart, you are storing up wrath against yourself for the day of God's* *wrath, when his **righteous judgment** will be revealed* (Romans 2:5).

This Judge deals with truth

Most countries have Courts where justice is meted out. Most of the very serious cases are dealt with in the major Courts. During trials, witnesses are put on oath to speak only the truth, but it is very doubtful as to whether the whole truth is told. In addition, the evidence against the accused may be flawed. But not at this Court. Jesus is the truth – ... *I am the way and **the truth** and the life. No-one comes to the Father except through me* (John 14:6). He only speaks truth, and He will make sure that everyone else does the same. How can the One who is truth tell lies? – *God is not a man, that he should lie, nor a son of man, that he should change his mind. Does he speak and then not act? Does he promise and not fulfil?* (Numbers 23:19). So, all justice on the great Day will be according to truth – *Now we know that God's judgment against those who do such things **is based on truth*** (Romans 2:2).

This Judge cannot be fooled

Men try to fool God, but it is not possible to do so. Man is no match for God; He is too wise to be fooled by men – *to the pure you show yourself pure, but to the crooked you show yourself shrewd* (2 Samuel 22:27). There have been many people who have duped their fellows in business deals, get-rich-quick schemes, and so on, but if they try their craftiness with God, they will find that He is more than a match for them – *He catches the wise in their craftiness, and the schemes of the wily are swept away* (Job 5:13). Some earthly judges can be influenced by bribes, and therefore criminals have escaped justice. But bribing God is impossible, in any case who could offer a sufficient bribe to the One who owns everything! – *Now let the fear of the LORD be upon you. Judge carefully, for with the LORD our God there is no injustice or partiality or bribery* (2 Chronicles 19:7). *For God does not show favouritism* (Romans 2:11).

The prisoners

The prisoners in the dock will be all those who rejected Jesus as their Saviour either deliberately, or by neglect. Jesus grieved greatly over their rejection while He was on earth; some of them were Israelites to whom He said – *O Jerusalem, Jerusalem, you who kill the prophets and stone those sent to you, how often I have longed to gather your children together, as a hen gathers her chicks under her wings, but you were not willing* (Matthew 23:37). But at the same time He made the consequences of their rejection very clear – *Whoever believes in the Son has eternal life, but whoever **rejects** the Son will not see life, for **God's wrath remains on him*** (John 3:36). He spoke the word of life to all mankind, and their response to that word decides the issue in the great Day – *There is a judge for the one who **rejects** me and does not accept my words; that very word which I spoke will condemn him at the last day* (John 12:48).

I believe that all these Christ rejectors are resurrected with their old body. All will be recognised according to their previous identity. These unforgiven sinners will be revolting to look at, because they did not receive the One who beautifies with salvation as in Scripture – *For the LORD takes delight in his people; he crowns* (beautifies) *the humble with salvation* (Psalm 149:4). Shorn of all the trappings of earth, they will have no credentials, robes, titles, or trappings. The records in the 'Books' mentioned in Revelation 20 are the only criteria there. The standard demanded is perfect righteousness.

The jailers

These seem to be unfallen Angels. There are many aspects to their work, and this is one of them – *The harvest is the end of the age, and **the harvesters are angels*** (Matthew 13:39). *And he will **send his angels** with a loud trumpet call, and they will gather his elect from the four winds, from one end of the Heavens to the other* (Matthew 24:31).

The Prosecutor

He is God the Holy Spirit. The One who convicts of sin. The Agent of the Godhead in the world – *When he comes, he will convict the world of guilt in regard to sin and righteousness and judgment* (John 16:8). He has a perfect memory – *But the Counsellor, the Holy Spirit, whom the Father will send in my name, will teach you all things and will remind you of everything I have said to you* (John 14:26). If He is able to remind Christians of all the things which Jesus said, He is able to recall all the evidence against the ungodly. His evidence will be complete, truthful, and damning.

The Judge's assistants

Christians are His assistants. They were judged at the Judgement Seat aspect of the Throne. Now they take their place with Jesus in this different aspect of His Throne – *Do you not know that the saints will judge the world? ... Do you not know that we will judge angels?* (1 Corinthians 6:2–3).

The Defence Counsel

Those who are saved had an Advocate or Counsel while they were on earth when they needed Him as such – *My dear children, I write this to you so that you will not sin. But if anybody does sin, we have one who speaks to the Father in our defence – Jesus Christ, the Righteous One* (1 John 2:1). On this occasion **they** do not need His Advocacy. As for the ungodly, their Judge cannot be their Advocate!

But there isn't one for the wicked

They could have had an Advocate while they were alive on earth. But they refused Him, now they cannot have His help. Some refused His help deliberately. God said to them: *All day long I have held out my hands to an obstinate people, who walk in ways not good, pursuing their own imaginations* (Isaiah 65:2); *yet you refuse to come to me to have life* (John

5:40). Others refused His help by neglect. God complained to His prophet Ezekiel in the Bible saying – *My people come to you, as they usually do, and sit before you to listen to your words, but they do not put them into practice. With their mouths they express devotion, but their hearts are greedy for unjust gain. Indeed, to them you are nothing more than one who sings love songs with a beautiful voice and plays an instrument well, for they hear your words but do not put them into practice* (Ezekiel 33:31–32). Isn't this rather like the common remark 'good sermon vicar'?

The evidence

The complete and accurate records of the lives of the ungodly will be read out in the hearing of all who have ever lived. The evidence includes every word the ungodly have ever spoken. Scripture is plain – *But I tell you that men will have to give account on the day of judgment for every careless word they have spoken. For by your words you will be acquitted, and by your words you will be condemned* (Matthew 12:36, 37).

It includes all they have ever done – *And I saw the dead, great and small, standing before the throne, and books were opened. Another book was opened, which is the book of life. The dead were judged according to what they had done as recorded in the books* (Revelation 20:12).

The verdict

Seeing that this occasion is the judgement of the ungodly, there is only one verdict given at this Throne – damnation, or as modern versions put it – condemnation. This verdict is a terrible one. Having separated the godly from the ungodly among the nations, God will utter His verdict to the ungodly – ...*Depart from me, you who are cursed, into the eternal fire prepared for the devil and his angels* (Matthew 25:41). The verdict has an eternal effect – *Let him who does wrong continue to do wrong; let him who is vile continue to be vile* (Revelation 22:11). Ungodly people will be set forever in the mould which they adopted in their earthly life.

The verdict is a fair one. God simply repays the ungodly, and He does it without spite. He cannot do otherwise – *Does God pervert justice? Does the Almighty pervert what is right?* (Job 8:3). *Thus **God repaid** the wickedness of Abimelech, which he had done to his father by killing his seventy brothers. And all the evil of the men of Shechem **God returned on their own heads**, and on them came the curse of Jotham the son of Jerubbaal* (Judges 9:56, 57 NKJV).

There is no mercy or grace at this Court

Because the Gospel age has gone by that time. There is plenty of mercy available now for all who want it, but it is unavailable then. This Great White Throne judgement does not include those who are born again. They will be at the Judgement Seat of Christ aspect of this Judgement Day.

The warning

Time after time God warns sinners to escape His anger and judgement. These included the religious leaders of His day. It is often the religious leaders who are more hard hearted than those whom they condemn as sinners, even in our time. Jesus, – *when he saw many of the Pharisees and Sadducees coming to where he was baptising, he said to them: 'You brood of vipers! Who warned you to **flee from the coming wrath?'** (Matthew 3:7).

If anyone reading this book is not a Christian, please run to God while you have a chance. Then you will find mercy and escape the terrors of Hell.

Some Christians find it hard to believe that God gets angry. So let us deal with it in the next chapter.

Chapter 21

The Anger of God

Hell is necessary so that God's anger can be expressed

God does get angry

But He only gets angry when it is necessary. He is also a God of love, but love without the element of anger is mere sentimentality. God is not sentimental – *because the Lord disciplines those he loves, and he punishes everyone he accepts as a son* (Hebrews 12:6). When we think of God's anger we must clearly distinguish between human and Divine anger. The one is not the same as the other. Human anger usually has malice in it, and loss of control. God's anger does not, for it is pure anger. Anger is either repressed or expressed; God does not repress His anger – *He will not always accuse, nor will he harbour his anger forever* (Psalm 103:9). The expression 'harbour anger' means in the Hebrew 'to cherish anger', or 'to bear a grudge'. Instead He pours out His anger and that is the end of the matter. While men are alive, God loves them – *For God so loved the world that he gave his one and only Son, that whoever believes in him shall not perish but have eternal life* (John 3:16). But if they reject His love His anger is aroused, and if they continue in their rejection, then His anger remains upon them forever – *Whoever believes in the Son*

202

has eternal life, but whoever rejects the Son will not see life, for God's wrath **remains** on him* (John 3:36).

God's anger does not alter His love. He is capable of expressing both emotions at the same time with equal strength. He never gets so angry that He forgets to be loving, but nor does ever become so loving that He overlooks sin. Consider these verses: firstly – *O LORD our God, you answered them; you were to Israel a **forgiving** God, though you **punished** their misdeeds* (Psalm 99:8). He loves enough to forgive, but is angry enough to punish when it is necessary. Another Scripture says – *But you, O Lord, are a compassionate and gracious God, slow to anger, abounding in **love*** and faithfulness (Psalms 86:15). God is slow to anger, but anger is there within Him, but it is alongside His love. He is still a loving God when He says – *Now leave me alone so that my anger may burn against them and that I may destroy them . . .* (Exodus 32:10). But He is so incensed with the nation's deliberate and awful sin, that He has to express His anger.

Causes of God's anger

The things which will make His anger permanent against those in Hell, are the things which they did on the earth. Because they did not repent of them on earth, they are punished for them forever. I mention them here so that, if we are guilty of these sins, we might repent of them, find forgiveness, and avoid the risk of God's eternal anger in Hell. Even if we are saved, we would do well to consider the following list, so that, if we are guilty of them we can repent while there is time and therefore not be ashamed when we meet Him.

Rebellion

*Remember this and never forget how you provoked the LORD your God to anger in the desert. From the day you left Egypt until you arrived here, you have been **rebellious** against the LORD* (Deuteronomy 9:7).

Disobedience

Because you did not obey the LORD or carry out his fierce wrath against the Amalekites, the LORD has done this to you today (1 Samuel 28:18). *Let no one deceive you with empty words, for because of such things God's anger comes on those who are disobedient* (Ephesians 5:6). Not only do people disobey God's Laws, they try to remove them. God likened His Laws to the property boundaries which were transgressed on pain of death – *'Cursed is the man who moves his neighbour's boundary stone.' Then all the people shall say, 'Amen!'* (Deuteronomy 27:17). *Judah's leaders are like those who move boundary stones. I will pour out my wrath on them like a flood of water* (Hosea 5:10).

Carelessness

The failure to remember who God is, and the rules He has laid down; the lack of godly fear are reasons why God pours out His anger both on earth and in hell. Uzzah was a careless Levite who should have known better than to take the sacred Ark and shove it on a cart, so – *The Lord's anger burned against Uzzah because of his irreverent act; therefore God struck him down and he died there beside the ark of God* (2 Samuel 6:7). Uzzah was a Levite and he knew very well that the Ark should have been carried with poles, not on a cart. David also knew the Law, so they were both guilty of the sin of carelessness.

Idolatry

Because they have forsaken me and burned incense to other gods and provoked me to anger by all the idols their hands have made, my anger will burn against this place and will not be quenched (2 Kings 22:17). If men worship strange gods, then God will make sure that they worship them forever – in Hell. There they will find out that their 'gods' were actually deceiving demons.

There is another form of idolatry which makes God angry – *Put to death, therefore, whatever belongs to your* *earthly nature: **sexual immorality**, impurity, lust, evil desires and greed, which is **idolatry. Because of these, the wrath of God is coming*** (Colossians 3:5, 6).

Mocking the messengers of God

But they mocked God's messengers, despised his words and scoffed at his prophets until the wrath of the LORD was aroused against his people and there was no remedy (2 Chronicles 36:16).

Profaning the Sabbath

Whether we regard Saturday or Sunday as the Sabbath it is important to regard one day in seven as devoted to the Lord – *Remember the Sabbath day by keeping it holy* (Exodus 20:8). Israel suffered for its disobedience to this commandment of God – *Didn't your forefathers do the same things, so that our God brought all this calamity upon us and upon this city? Now you are stirring up more anger against Israel by desecrating the Sabbath* (Nehemiah 13:18). So will we if we ignore God's day in order to shop more conveniently with Sunday trading.

There are so many ways in which we can arouse the anger of God. Scripture gives us a list as well as those above – *Put to death, therefore, whatever belongs to your earthly nature: sexual immorality, impurity, lust, evil desires and greed, which is idolatry. Because of these, the wrath of God is coming* (Colossians 3:5, 6). There are even more in another Epistle – *idolatry and witchcraft; hatred, discord, jealousy, fits of rage, selfish ambition, dissensions, factions and envy; drunkenness, orgies, and the like. I warn you, as I did before, that those who live like this will not inherit the kingdom of God* (Galatians 5:20–21). If people persist in these sins they will experience the anger of God forever. It is not worth the risk!

The major crime against God

And yet, none of these things are as bad as the major crime

committed by mankind. This crime is that of rejecting Jesus, the only Saviour. If the greatest commandment is to – ... *Love the Lord your God with all your heart and with all your soul and with all your mind* (Matthew 22:37), then the greatest crime is to refuse to do so. Loving Him wholeheartedly, is the evidence that we are born again and that we have accepted Him as **Lord**? If we love Him, we obey Him.

God's anger here and now

God shows His anger even before the great Day of judgement. He gives timely reminders on earth that He is not a God to be trifled with. If only people would understand! We must not think that every earthly tragedy is an expression of God's anger. But when Israel sinned continuously against God, he did show His anger against them – *He unleashed against them his hot wrath, his anger, indignation and hostility – a band of destroying angels* (Psalm 78:49). So, angelic powers apply God's anger sometimes, for all of them whether good or evil are under His control. The ungodly cannot escape the effects of God's anger, and sometimes the righteous suffer with the unrighteous for example:

Droughts

Droughts are often the result of man's misuse of the earth. If people insist on chopping down trees, then the unprotected earth will turn to dust and cease to be cultivatable. The Sahara was once the breadbasket of the Roman empire remember. On other occasions God causes them in order to show His anger – *Then the Lord's anger will burn against you, and he will shut the heavens so that it will **not rain** and the ground will yield no produce, and you will soon perish from the good land the* LORD *is giving you* (Deuteronomy 11:17).

Displacement

If a nation ignores God's repeated warnings, he will do

drastic things such as uprooting the nation and banishing them elsewhere – *In furious anger and in great wrath the* LORD **uprooted them** *from their land and thrust them into another land, as it is now* (Deuteronomy 29:28).

However, these manifestations of His anger are only a foretaste; in the Day of judgement, God's anger will be poured out fully and finally on all who have disobeyed Him. No wonder the Bible urges us to ...*flee from the coming wrath* (Luke 3:7). The Bible points us to ... *Jesus, who rescues us from the coming wrath* (1 Thessalonians 1:10). He rescues us – but only if we let Him do so while we are alive. At all costs let us run to Him while we can.

Effects of His anger in Hell

The foretaste of His anger which we may experience on earth leads to the fulfilment of it in Hell where God expresses His anger eternally. The sins I have mentioned above do not leave God unmoved, and he cannot turn a blind eye to them; if He did, He would not be a righteous God. Sin arouses God's anger and brings it upon those who persist in them. If such sins are not confessed and forgiven, those who commit them reap the awful consequences. Sin will be punished on the Day of Judgement when God's anger is manifested against them, but the carrying out of the sentence will take place in Hell where there is an unending experience of His anger, but with no opportunity to cry for His mercy – *Whoever believes in the Son has eternal life, but whoever rejects the Son will not see life, for God's wrath* **remains** *on him* (John 3:36).

There is an eternal experience of His silence in Hell for God has nothing to say to the occupants. He said it all before, through the Bible. It is a dreadful thing to experience God's silence. That is why David the Psalmist said – *To you I call, O* LORD *my Rock; do not turn a deaf ear to me. For if you remain silent, I will be like those who have gone down to the pit* (Psalm 28:1).

May God help us to be more faithful in warning people to escape this dreadful experience while they can do so. God's anger leads to punishment . . .

Chapter 22

God's Punishment of Sin

Hell is needed because punishment is deserved

God's anger leads to God's punishment – unless there is repentance. Just punishment preserves society's order and it helps to prevent anarchy. It instils a sense of right and wrong in our children. Proper punishment must fit the crime. It is not enough to sentence drunken drivers who kill to Community service or to fine them a derisory sum of money. Children who badly injure disabled pensioners need to be punished severely so that they will learn a lesson and not be so cowardly again. Those who rail against the principle of punishment are usually evildoers, or they are guilty of mere sentimentality. Judges and magistrates who refuse to impose proper penalties are guilty before God and will have to give an account when they stand before Him. Some modern sociologists will doubtless talk about draconian penalties, and the need to be tolerant to criminals, but the Bible has no time for such nonsense. In fact God's decree that *Whoever sheds the blood of man, by man shall his blood be shed; for in the image of God has God made man* (Genesis 9:6), has never been repealed. The authorities should be mindful of this, and more church leaders should preach it.

God punishes sin on earth

God mainly punishes sin in Hell as the Bible says – *Then*

*they will go away to eternal **punishment**, but the righteous to eternal life* (Matthew 25:46). *In a similar way, Sodom and Gomorrah and the surrounding towns gave themselves up to sexual immorality and perversion. They serve as an example of those who suffer the **punishment** of eternal fire* (Jude 1:7). But God does punish sin to some extent on the earth, although at times it seems that ungodly people get away with their evil deeds on the earth. We hear reports of murder and carnage every day in our news bulletins. God does seem to be inactive in the face of so much crime in the world. But if we think carefully, God does intervene, even though He seems to be slow about it. Israel was cruelly treated by the surrounding nations time after time. In fact God allowed it on occasions. But when Habbakuk cried out to God about the cruelty of the Chaldeans – *How long, O LORD, must I call for help, but you do not listen? Or cry out to you, 'Violence!' but you do not save?* (Habakkuk 1:2), God replied and acted to crush those who were crushing Israel. The whole of Habbakuk chapter 2 shows this to be true.

Some brief examples of the things which God punished on earth are –

Cruelty

Some nations such as the Amalekites seem to get away with cruelty for a long time, but, although God is patient, His patience has limits. When that limit is reached, let nations beware – *This is what the LORD Almighty says: 'I will punish the Amalekites for what they did to Israel when they waylaid them as they came up from Egypt* (1Samuel 15:2). The Egyptians were cruel to the Israelites when they put them to forced labour, and when they tried to kill all the baby boys. God seemed to be silent for a long while, but when He did punish Egypt, it was a drastic punishment. Exodus chapters 6 to 11 tell the story. Why not read it!

Disobedience

God sets a high value on obedience. In fact it is one of the requirements of salvation – *Whoever believes in the Son has eternal life, but whoever rejects* (disobeys) *the Son will not see life, for God's wrath remains on him* (John 3:36). One reason why God led the Israelites through the wilderness, facing them with many dangerous situations is described in Scripture – *They were left to test the Israelites to see whether they would **obey** the Lord's commands, which he had given their forefathers through Moses* (Judges 3:4). Obviously then His punishment of disobedience is severe – *Whoever does not **obey** the law of your God and the law of the king must surely be punished by death, banishment, confiscation of property, or imprisonment* (Ezra 7:26).

Pride and ruthlessness

This world is full of ruthless people who crush others under their feet as they build their empires, whether the empire is territorial or commercial. Ungodly kings, emperors, Presidents, multinational directors, and gangsters – all will be punished by God, sometimes while they are on earth, but certainly in the great Day – *I will punish the world for its evil, the wicked for their sins. I will put an end to the arrogance of the haughty and will humble the pride of the ruthless* (Isaiah 13:11).

Bad leaders

The world's leaders in particular will have to give account of the way in which they exercised the privilege of leading God's nations. They must remember that – *The earth is the Lord's, and everything in it, the world, and all who live in it* (Psalm 24:1). If they fail in their duty to lead in a godly way they will suffer in the great Day. Leadership involves stewardship, and stewards, whoever they are must give account to God. The church is not guiltless in the matter of bad leadership. Those Bishops who deny the Faith and encourage compromise to the Law of God will be punished with greater severity than some of the world's criminals – *Not many of you should presume to be teachers, my brothers, because you know that we who teach will be judged more strictly* (James 3:1).

Jesus, the head of the Church said – *My anger burns against the shepherds, and I will punish the leaders; for the* LORD *Almighty will care for his flock, the house of Judah, and make them like a proud horse in battle* (Zechariah 10:3).

Love and punishment are not contradictory

I said in chapter 21 – 'The Anger of God' that God's anger does not alter His love; similarly His love does not contradict His punishment. There are always some sentimentalists who say that we should not punish people and nor should we be hard on children because they must be allowed to do what they like and express themselves. Having been a City Missionary in Liverpool I know what the little dears like doing. They like throwing bricks through Chapel windows! God, in His healthy robust way says – *Do not withhold discipline from a child; if you punish him with the rod, he will not die* (Proverbs 23:13). In extreme cases God is extreme – *If a man has a stubborn and rebellious son who does not obey his father and mother and will not listen to them when they discipline him, his father and mother shall take hold of him and bring him to the elders at the gate of his town. They shall say to the elders, 'This son of ours is stubborn and rebellious. He will not obey us. He is a profligate and a drunkard.' Then all the men of his town shall stone him to death. You must purge the evil from among you. All Israel will hear of it and be afraid* (Deuteronomy 21:18–21). Such punishment would seem excessive today, even to Christian parents, but if God does not change, His views on discipline are the same today. Somehow or other we must share His concern. God loves His children, and because His love is not sentimental He punishes them when they need it – *because the Lord disciplines those he loves, and he punishes everyone he accepts as a son* (Hebrews 12:6). The word 'chasten' actually means applying all those firm and helpful things which enable a child to grow up and mature, so it is not cruel at all. Let us remember that God's loving purpose in punishing some people on earth was to safeguard the rest.

This is the age of mercy

For he says, 'In the time of my favour I heard you, and in the day of salvation I helped you.' I tell you, **now is the time of God's favour***, now is the day of salvation* (2 Corinthians 6:2). There is mercy in God's punishment, at least for those who are alive on earth at the moment. Ezra knew this and wrote about it – *What has happened to us is a result of our evil deeds and our great guilt, and yet, our God, you have punished us less than our sins have deserved and have given us a remnant like this* (Ezra 9:13). Paul was a balanced writer, and he put the two together in his writings – *For the wages of sin is death, but* **the gift of God** *is eternal life in Christ Jesus our Lord* (Romans 6:23). Consider how patient God is. The whole world must be a stench in His nostrils; sin abounds; men get more and more wicked, and yet He waits for sinners to repent and escape eternal punishment – *The Lord is not slow in keeping his promise, as some understand slowness. He is patient with you, not wanting anyone to perish, but everyone to come to repentance* (2 Peter 3:9). *The* LORD *is slow to anger, abounding in love and forgiving sin and rebellion* (Numbers 14:18).

There are degrees of punishment in Hell

I have already explained that God is a fair and righteous Judge. Therefore he will not punish ordinary citizens in the same way as He punishes tyrants such as Nero, Pharaoh, Hitler, Hussein. Scripture explains this principle – *That servant who knows his master's will and does not get ready or does not do what his master wants will be beaten with many blows. But the one who does not know and does things deserving punishment will be beaten with few blows. From everyone who has been given much, much will be demanded; and from the one who has been entrusted with much, much more will be asked* (Luke 12:47–48). *But it will be more bearable for Tyre and Sidon at the judgment than for you* (Luke 10:14). Because all punishment in Hell is awful, to write about the degree of it may seem academic, but I do so in order to show how scrupulously fair God is in His punishment of sin.

Having said that, we must go on to say that if the greatest command is to – *Love the Lord your God with all your heart and with all your soul and with all your mind* (Matthew 22:37), then the greatest sin must be to disobey it. Also, if Jesus went to such lengths to bring us salvation, then the greatest insult we can offer to God is to refuse or neglect it. Scripture puts this very graphically – *How much more severely do you think a man deserves to be punished who has trampled the Son of God under foot, who has treated as an unholy thing the blood of the covenant that sanctified him, and who has insulted the Spirit of grace?* (Hebrews 10:29).

The degrees of punishment are degrees of **intensity**, not just **duration** (duration is the same for all, i.e. eternal).

An objection to eternal punishment

Some say 'if the punishment for sin was put on Jesus at Calvary, why is there a need for eternal punishment?' Jesus certainly suffered the complete punishment for the sin of the world – *He is the atoning sacrifice for our sins, and not only for ours but also for the sins of the whole world* (1 John 2:2). But this atonement opened the way for deliverance for **all who availed themselves of it** while there was time. It did not bring about universal salvation. Those who rejected Jesus, are still liable for the punishment of their unforgiven sins. Others say that eternal punishment for man's 70 years of sin is unjust.

In earthly courts the length of time taken to commit crime has no bearing on the severity of the sentence. Only God can properly estimate sin's vileness. Only He is free from sin, therefore the only pure and dispassionate Judge of it. There are some who say that an eternal punishment for a mere lifetime of sin is unfair. They say that God would be more fair if He just punished sinners for a short time and then annihilated them. Sadly for them, the Bible says that punishment is eternal. No one can argue with the only God. Eternal existence means eternal existence. Let me enlarge on the word eternal...

Chapter 23

Hell is Eternal

People still exist on the Day of Judgement

There is no such thing as annihilation. No one disappears at their death. Among the texts which prove this are – *And I saw the dead, great and small, standing before the throne, and books were opened. Another book was opened, which is the book of life. The dead were judged according to what they had done as recorded in the books. The sea gave up the dead that were in it, and death and Hades gave up the dead that were in them, and each person was judged according to what he had done* (Revelation 20:12, 13).

People also exist *after* that Day

A number of Scriptures also show that people exist **after** the Day of Judgement. They are not **living** as Christians are in Heaven, but are **existing** and still conscious. They are not thrown into oblivion, but into prison – *And throw that worthless servant outside, into the darkness, where there will be weeping and gnashing of teeth* (Matthew 25:30). *Then he will say to those on his left, 'Depart from me, you who are cursed, into the eternal fire prepared for the devil and his angels* (Matthew 25:41). *In hell, where he was in torment, he looked up and saw Abraham far away, with Lazarus by his* *side* (Luke 16:23). This is not a depiction of **living**, but mere awful **existence**. However, it is a proof that they are alive. The Scriptures speak of eternal destruction, and of perishing eternally. The words need some explanation.

Eternal destruction

*They will be punished with **everlasting destruction*** (Greek: 'olethros') *and shut out from the presence of the Lord and from the majesty of his power* (2 Thessalonians 1:9). Everlasting destruction sounds like a contradiction in terms. How can something be eternal if it is destroyed? The problem lies in the translation of Greek terms into English. 'Destruction', in English generally means that something which once existed not longer exists; it is gone. However, in Greek the word 'destroy' or 'destruction' means loss of well-being; ruined; wasted; spoiled. Some Scriptures illustrate the point – *Since the children have flesh and blood, he too shared in their humanity so that by his death he might **destroy*** (Greek: 'katargeo') *him who holds the power of death – that is, the devil* (Hebrews 2:14). *By the same word the present heavens and earth are reserved for fire, being kept for the day of judgment and destruction* (Greek: 'apoleia' – waste, ruin) *of ungodly men* (2 Peter 3:7).

Eternal perishing

Again, there seems to be a contradiction, for the same reason. The word 'perished' used in Greek means something made void or useless. Something or someone reduced to inactivity. The words 'destruction' and 'perishing' are virtually interchangeable. But neither word means that someone is literally destroyed or perished. Consider some Scriptures where these terms are used – *And the LORD did this. Dense swarms of flies poured into Pharaoh's palace and into the houses of his officials, and throughout Egypt the land was ruined by the flies* (Exodus 8:24). **Egypt was not literally**

destroyed. *You are destroyed, O Israel, because you are against me, against your helper* (Hosea 13:9). **Israel was not literally destroyed.** *Jesus answered them, 'Destroy this temple, and I will raise it again in three days'* (John 2:19). *But the temple he had spoken of was his body* (John 2:21). **Jesus was not literally destroyed.** *Since the children have flesh and blood, he too shared in their humanity so that by his death he might destroy him who holds the power of death – that is, the devil* (Hebrews 2:14). **Satan was not literally destroyed**.

So, Destruction (or perishing) is an eternal process

Destruction (or perishing) is not a 'once for all' event. Nor is it a process which has an eventual end when a being ceases to exist. It is an everlasting process. It happens in a place where people are always dying, but find it is impossible to die! *The soul who sins is the one who will die* (Ezekiel 18:20). The soul or spirit is the eternal part of man. It cannot 'die' as in physical death; it 'dies' in the sense of separation from God – *Do not be afraid of those who kill the body but cannot kill the soul. Rather, be afraid of the One who can destroy* (Greek: 'appolumi') *both soul and body in hell* (Matthew 10:28).

The words 'destruction', or 'perishing' do not mean exclusion from existence, but exclusion from the presence of the Lord. This exclusion is eternal, and the state of the lost is eternal. Our physical death seals a decision made about our eternal destiny before we die. Our condition after death is final, and fixed. Scripture is dogmatic about this – *Let him who does wrong continue to do wrong; let him who is vile continue to be vile; let him who does right continue to do right; and let him who is holy continue to be holy* (Revelation 22:11). God has nothing more to do or say in the matter of man's destiny. Is there any point in studying these unpleasant doctrines? Yes – because of the needs of the heathen...

Chapter 24

The Heathen

Who are the heathen?

If someone does not become born again, surrendering their whole life to Jesus Christ, they are heathen. Heathen are not only the illiterate savages in the jungle, but include those who are literate and civilised but who do not worship God. None are without some understanding of right and wrong. To some extent all peoples have the light of God. The Bible declares that – *The true light that gives light to every man was coming into the world* (John 1:9). That light might be dim in some areas of the world, but it is there. Consider the following facts in Scriptures –

All have the light of Creation

If we take the trouble to look at Creation in all its forms – oceans, lakes, rivers, rain, snow, trees, plants, mountains, minerals, stars, planets, and so on – we cannot fail to detect a great Hand or Mind behind it all. God shows Himself through these wonderful aspects of Creation. Scripture says so – *Yet he has not left himself without testimony: He has shown kindness by giving you rain from heaven and crops in their seasons; he provides you with plenty of food and fills your hearts with joy* (Acts 14:17). Again Scripture says – *since what may be known about God is plain to them, because*

God has made it plain to them. For since the creation of the world God's invisible qualities – his eternal power and divine nature – have been clearly seen, being understood from what has been made, **so that men are without excuse** (Romans 1:19–20).

All have the light of conscience

No one anywhere is without some knowledge of truth. The Bible makes this plain – *The wrath of God is being revealed from heaven against all the godlessness and wickedness of men who* **suppress the truth** *by their wickedness* (Romans 1:18). They must know truth otherwise they could not suppress it! The heathen, be they savages in the jungle or well-clad people in 'civilisation' have some understanding of God – *For although they* **knew God***, they neither glorified him as God nor gave thanks to him, but their thinking became futile and their foolish hearts were darkened* (Romans 1:21). Again Scripture says this – *(Indeed, when Gentiles, who do not have the law, do by nature things required by the law, they are a law for themselves, even though they do not have the law, since they show that the requirements of the law are written on their hearts, their consciences also bearing witness, and their thoughts now accusing, now even defending them.)* (Romans 2:14–15).

The standards of the heathen may be false standards, but they have **some** understanding, therefore they are not without responsibility. Ignorance may lessen guilt, but it cannot nullify it. Even Stone Age tribes know the difference between right and wrong. A missionary in the former Congo asked the leader of such a tribe to name things which were sin the answer came without hesitation – 'witchcraft, murder, theft and adultery'. So, in the light of these Scriptures we must say that whoever and whatever people are in the world, all are responsible to live up to the light they have. None are free from responsibility. However I illustrate an important point from Scripture –

There are degrees of responsibility

*Since you call on a Father who judges **each man's work impartially**, live your lives as strangers here in reverent fear* (1 Peter 1:17). *That servant who knows his master's will and does not get ready or does not do what his master wants will be beaten with **many blows**. But the one who does not know and does things deserving punishment will be beaten with **few blows**. From everyone who has been given much, much will be demanded; and from the one who has been entrusted with much, much more will be asked* (Luke 12:47–48). But remember that a lesser degree of responsibility does not nullify guilt or deliver anyone from the just judgement or punishment for sin.

All Judgement will be fair and according to truth

Far be it from you to do such a thing – to kill the righteous with the wicked, treating the righteous and the wicked alike. Far be it from you! Will not the Judge of all the earth do right? (Genesis 18:25). And again – *Now we know that God's judgment against those who do such things is based on **truth*** (Romans 2:2).

I write more about righteous judgement in chapter 20 – 'The Judgement Day'.

What about the unevangelised?

The question is often asked 'what about those who did not hear the Gospel?' I confess that I am not altogether clear about the answer, but I would make some observations about it. Firstly, I do not believe in Universalism (the view that all are saved eventually). This doctrine minimises the seriousness of sin and cheapens Calvary. I write more about Universalism in chapter 2 – 'Who will be in Heaven?' and chapter 5 – 'What is Heaven Like?'Secondly, there is no middle ground regarding sin. Men are either righteous or wicked. Thirdly, no one is saved except through Jesus. Fourthly, the heathen are responsible for their actions whether they are regarded as Stone Age or civilised.

The unsaved heathen are lost

But why? Because God regards them as sinners – *for all have sinned and fall short of the glory of God* (Romans 3:23). And therefore – *the wages of sin is death...* (Romans 6:23). They are not lost just because they are unevangelised, they are lost because condemnation comes through guilt not through ignorance. They are sinners, therefore they are guilty before God. If, as some say, they are not lost, then the Coming, sacrifice, and resurrection of Christ is irrelevant. It would be a bold man to say that! Even the avowed atheist Tom Paine said at his death 'Oh, Christ help me! It is Hell to be left alone.' The last words of the atheist Voltaire were 'I shall go to Hell, O Jesus Christ.' There are not many real atheists on a death bed!

Is there any hope for them apart from Jesus?

Try as I might, I can find no evidence in Scripture that anyone is saved except by faith in Jesus and total surrender to Him. Consider the Scriptures – *Salvation is found in no-one else, for there is **no other name** under heaven given to men by which we must be saved* (Acts 4:12). Jesus said – *I am the way and the truth and the life. No-one comes to the Father except through me* (John 14:6). This is the holy dogmatism that enrages those of other religions, but Jesus is God, and He has the right to be dogmatic. What other god is greater than Him with a right to overrule what he says? Away with the tolerance of some theologians. Let Christians be as bold and dogmatic as Jesus was. To suggest, as some do, that we leave the heathen alone would seem to indicate that the Gospel has nothing to offer them. It has – and we must not leave them alone. What a need for missionaries! Those who will faithfully warn of the terrors of Hell. Is mission work on the decline these days I wonder? Mission work includes preaching the Gospel....

Chapter 25

Preach the Gospel

God does not accept any excuses for not preaching the Gospel

Imagine a doctor who went out to a country where a plague was raging. He had a plentiful supply of medicine with which to combat that plague. As he got nearer to the dying people, he got distracted by some beautiful plants nearby, and spent time smelling their fragrance. Then, although he was not far from the people, he decided that he needed a rest, so he had a nap. Then, having seen the state of them, he said to himself, 'I am rather a shy person, so perhaps I ought to keep away.' Eventually he did go to the people and wandered around uttering sympathetic words to the children who were sitting by the corpses of their parents, and patting the head of a man near to death who was surrounded by the bodies of his entire family. If he did all this, but neglected to give any injections from his supply of lifesaving drugs, what would you think of him? Would he be thoughtless, lazy, or callous? Yes. But even worse, he would be a murderer. He had the ability to save lives, but he did not do so. He had the only remedy for that plague but he withheld it from those who were dying through lack of it. This is an imaginary incident, but it does illustrate selfish Christians who do not bother with those who are dying from a deadly disease called sin. If we are in that category, then we are disobeying the Lord whom we profess to love. He said – ... *Go into all the world and preach the good news to all creation* (Mark 16:15). God also uttered this stern warning to us – *When I say to the wicked, 'O wicked man, you will surely die,' and you do not speak out to dissuade him from his ways, that wicked man will die for his sin, and I will hold you accountable for his blood* (Ezekiel 33:8). Will we have blood on our hands when we stand at the Throne? Perhaps – but we need not have, if we are faithful in witnessing and preaching the Gospel.

We need to be dogmatic

I am disgusted with the attitude in which some churchmen speak sentimentally about other Faiths. They try to be very accommodating to them, and there are even some Christians who say that there may be other ways to God apart from the Gospel. It is true that we must show the love of God to those of other Faiths, but in doing so, we must never compromise in our preaching of the Gospel. It is not easy to be dogmatic, and there is an art in speaking strongly and yet with the grace of Jesus. God help us to learn it!

Jesus was dogmatic

John says that Jesus was – ... *full of grace and truth* (John 1:14). Not so gracious that He forgot to be truthful; and not so truthful that He forgot to be gracious. He did not hesitate to be direct in His preaching, and He made tremendous claims for Himself (all of which were true). He plainly said – ... *I am the way and the truth and the life. No one comes to the Father except through me* (John 14:6). He spoke the truth – there is no other way of salvation! He did not waste time in arguing, unlike so much of today's 'dialogue'. He was a Man in a hurry; He had no time to waste. He said – *As long as it is day, we must do the work of him who sent me. Night is coming, when no-one can work* (John 9:4). There was a divine urgency in Jesus: let the Spirit of God create it in us. He will do so, if we stop having dialogue and get on with the job of preaching the Gospel.

The disciples were dogmatic

When Peter was changed from a coward into a zealot God began to use him to preach the Gospel. (If God could change Peter, He can change anyone, including you.) The Bible rightly says that – *Fear of man will prove to be a snare* (Proverbs 29:25). How many people are in Hell now because Christians were afraid to speak to them, claiming to 'be shy'? Shyness has to be conquered, and we need to get the blood of those whom we have not shared the Gospel with off our hands **quickly**. Peter spoke with holy boldness and dogmatism when he said – *Salvation is found in no one else, for there is no other name under heaven given to men by which we must be saved* (Acts 4:12). If God could change cowardly Peter, He can change us. Why not let Him?

This majestic dogmatism of God and His people is offensive to those who reject Him, but there is no valid argument when it is the Sovereign God who preaches the message of salvation. You take it, or leave it. But eternal consequences stem from our action. Life down here can be likened to a probation, or a preparation; an opportunity to choose life or death.

Scripture demands that we preach the whole Gospel

Paul did not believe in half measures, he said – *For I have not hesitated to proclaim to you the whole will of God* (Acts 20:27). The whole 'will' includes the whole Gospel, not parts of it. It includes the teaching on Heaven and Hell. Both truths are vital, and must not be excluded. Other aspects of the Gospel are – The Atonement; The Resurrection; Justification by faith; Repentance; Faith; Transformation. We are not likely to include all theses aspects during a 'gossiping the Gospel' session in the supermarket, but it is important that we know them so that we can give a clear message when we get the chance.

Two of God's major objectives in sending Jesus to die and rise again were to save mankind from eternal grief and ruin (perishing), and to welcome Him into the eternal joy and wholeness of Heaven. If the Gospel is good news, and it is, then we must learn the whole of it, and then preach the whole of it. God have mercy on those who abbreviate it. Remember that searing Scripture – *I warn everyone who hears the words of the prophecy of this book: If anyone adds anything to them, God will add to him the plagues described in this book. And if anyone takes words away from this book of prophecy, God will take away from him his share in the tree of life and in the holy city, which are described in this book* (Revelation 22:18, 19).

It is a comforting Gospel

The Gospel we preach is the only Gospel which offers forgiveness, joy, peace, and an eternal Home. I hope that the description I have given of Heaven should convince us of that. Other religions make terrible demands on their followers, even that of human sacrifice, at least in olden times, although there are disturbing reports of human sacrifice today. I for one would not discount them because Satan's tactics are no different from those he used in olden times. Satan is not creative!

It is a demanding Gospel

God also makes demands on His followers, but they are demands which lead to safety in this life and the next. Firstly, God demands total surrender from all who would receive His salvation – *Therefore, I urge you, brothers, in view of God's mercy, to offer your bodies as living sacrifices, holy and pleasing to God – this is your spiritual act of worship. Do not conform any longer to the pattern of this world, but be transformed by the renewing of your mind. Then you will be able to test and approve what God's will is – his good, pleasing and perfect will* (Romans 12:1–2). But He has the right to make these demands; firstly because of His right as our Creator – *For every living soul belongs to me, the father as well as the son – both alike belong to me. The soul who sins is the one who will die* (Ezekiel 18:4).

Secondly, because He has given us everything He has except His deity, He expects us to give Him everything we have. *He who did not spare his own Son, but gave him up for us all – how will he not also, along with him, graciously give us all things?* (Romans 8:32). In the light of God's wholehearted giving to us, we must surely give Him everything we have!

Therefore we must never water down the Gospel we preach. I have led a number of men to the Lord, and the 'preaching' has been very straight and brief. It went like this – 'Sir, if you and I drop dead in a few minutes time, I will go to Heaven, and you will go to Hell. Secondly, you have broken God's Laws and you must cry for mercy. Thirdly, if you want to be a Christian, you must totally surrender your life to Him. So, sir, please yourself what you do.' Most of them responded, and are in the Kingdom today. Please understand that I knew what the Holy Spirit wanted me to do on these occasions; it was not done in a careless fashion. Please also remember that it does not always happen this way!

Sacrifice, surrender, and obedience

These are major truths which must be preached. The essence of sin is disobedience. The heart of the Gospel is God's requirement of obedience and faith. It is of major importance then, that people should decide to receive **and obey** the Son of God. Our attitude to Him decides our eternal future – *Whoever believes in the Son has eternal life, but whoever rejects the Son will not see life, for God's wrath remains on him* (John 3:36). The NASB version of the Bible uses the words *does not obey* instead of the NIV words *whoever rejects*. I think it emphasises something very important.

The book of Leviticus can be a hard book to read. The constant detailed instructions about sacrifice and offerings can make one wonder why God required all these details. The severe punishment for failing to offer them underlines the serious view God takes of sin, or robbing God which is the same thing. To obey God always demands sacrifice – the sacrificing of what I want to do, in order to do what He wants me to do. Leviticus foreshadows Calvary where God showed finally what He feels about transgression or dis-obedience. The book also shows that God also takes a high view of obedience. Calvary again is the great revelation of the perfect obedience God required in the Lamb who took away the sin of the world. Thank God for the obedience of Jesus.

It is a transforming Gospel

The Bible points out that regeneration should make a com-plete difference to our life – *Therefore, if anyone is in Christ,* **he is a new creation; the old has gone**, *the new has come!* (2 Corinthians 5:17). If we are born again, we need not, and we must not live as we did before. God uses the picture of light and darkness to illustrate it. Light is an enemy of darkness – it dispels it – *For you were once darkness, but now you are light in the Lord. Live as children of light* (Ephe-sians 5:8). God also points out that it is a matter of chang-ing kingdoms. From that of Satan to God's great Kingdom – *to open their eyes and turn them* **from darkness to light**, *and from the power of Satan to God, so that they may receive forgiveness of sins and a place among those who are sancti-fied by faith in me* (Acts 26:18). Many, though not all of those who constantly ask for counselling waste the time of leaders who should be engaged primarily in warfare. The only real justification for spiritual counselling is to keep the troops fit for spiritual warfare.

Much of today's Gospel preaching is sloppy, semi-bibli-cal, and, quite frankly, preached with a view to counting heads afterwards. Jesus never preached an easy Gospel, nor was His desire to simply help mankind to have a happy trouble free life on earth. In many of today's sermons there is little if any emphasis on sacrifice, surrender, and transformation. Faulty Gospel preaching will produce faulty 'Christians'. This means that not all who profess to be Christians are truly born again. Those who preach a faulty Gospel tremble on the brink of blasphemy. They misrepresent God if they fail to preach His demands for transformation as well as His love. I repeat that Gospel preaching is incomplete without the mention of these important aspects of it.

Not all those who profess to being saved are really born again. Furthermore, Those who preach only the love of God tremble on the brink of blasphemy. They misrepresent God if they fail to preach His holiness and judgement as well as His love. I repeat that Gospel preaching is incomplete without the mention of Heaven and Hell, as well as the subjects above. Two of God's major objectives in sending Jesus to die and rise again were to save mankind from eternal grief and ruin (perishing), and to welcome him into the eternal joy and wholeness of Heaven. If the Gospel is good news, and it is, then we must learn the whole of it, and then preach the whole of it. God have mercy on those who abbreviate it. Remember that searing Scripture – *I warn everyone who hears the words of the prophecy of this book: If anyone adds anything to them, God will add to him the plagues described in this book. And if anyone takes words away from this book of prophecy, God will take away from him his share in the tree of life and in the holy city, which are described in this book* (Revelation 22:18–19).

Why preach the Gospel?

Because Jesus did

One of the most important reasons why we should preach the whole of the Gospel message is that **Jesus did so**. He is our Master, and we are His servants; so we must heed the injunction – *A student is not above his teacher, but everyone who is fully trained will be like his teacher* (Luke 6:40). Therefore we must preach the Gospel as He did, and preach it as thoroughly as He did.

Because Jesus commands us to do so

Therefore go and make disciples of all nations, baptising them in the name of the Father and of the Son and of the Holy Spirit (Matthew 28:19). He did not advocate endless committee meetings about going, He said **'go'**. Remember that Jesus is looking at us, longing that souls should be saved through our preaching, expecting that our love for Him, and our gratitude to Him will urge us on to give Him the desires of His heart.

Because of rampant sin

Another reason for preaching the Gospel is the fact that sin is so widespread. Satan is enraged because his time is short; he stops at nothing to enslave mankind while he can. We must stop at nothing to defeat him, by halting the progress of sin. We can do it – with the Gospel!

Because so many people are in danger

We know that we are children of God, and that the whole world is under the control of the evil one (1 John 5:19). The NIV is a bad translation of this verse, so I quote from another translation – *We know that we are of God, and the whole world lies **under the sway** of the wicked one* (1 John 5:19 NKJV). **God** is in control of this world, but Satan certainly has a lot of **sway**. However, my main point is that there are many many people who need the Gospel. They are in danger of eternal separation from God, and eternal judgement, and the wrath of God – *Whoever believes in the Son has eternal life, but whoever rejects the Son will not see life, for **God's wrath remains on him*** (John 3:36). *For the wages of sin is **death**, but the gift of God is eternal life in Christ Jesus our Lord* (Romans 6:23). Do we care? If so, what action will we take?

To show that we care

We need to counter our apathy. How can Christians be apathetic when the world is going to Hell? Why is mission so unpopular these days? Why is sin so rampant? The answer lies partly in the fact that the church has neglected the doctrine of Hell. No one who meditates on its horrors can be apathetic in evangelism. So let us meditate on Heaven and Hell while we can. Let us learn to pray as never before. *Lord, teach us to pray.* E.M. Bounds wrote:

> 'We pray powerfully when we feel deeply.'
> (*Power through Prayer*. E.M. Bounds)

Let us preach as never before. As someone said – 'let us preach as dying men to dying men.' We need to weep more than we do. Please read Appendix 2. It is one of the most motivating things I have read. It taught me to weep, and to reach out to the lost. May God make us better stewards of the Gospel. We need to value souls as God does. 'Lord, teach me the value of a soul.'

What is the point of this book? Let me try to answer the question . . .

Finally

Contemplation of Heaven brings results

I hope that you are as thrilled about Heaven as I am. Whether it is the Kingdom aspect of Heaven, or the Rewards, or the Wedding, or the Coming, it is all so exciting and wonderful. I can hardly wait to get there. Do you feel the same? When we talk about Heaven we are not talking about 'pie in the sky' stuff. We have no time for unreality. But if Heaven is real to us, we will make time to think about it.

It increases our anticipation

If someone emigrated to a far off country in time past, when travel was nowhere near as easy as it is today, they were usually there for good. But they would not forget their home and their loved ones. They would get on with their work, and the years would go by, but home would often be in their thoughts. In their view there was no other place quite like their home town, and they would hope to be back there at some stage in their life. These thoughts are not an exact parallel to our subject because we have not lived in Heaven yet, and therefore have not left it, but surely it has some similarity to our attitude towards our real Home in Heaven. For a Christian it is natural to think of the time when they go to their proper Home, to meet with those who are dear to them. Especially to their beloved Father God. As we contemplate the glories of Heaven, things get put into perspective. Among them are the following –

It puts suffering and testing in context

Suffering of one sort or another is the experience of most people. In some countries Christians are suffering persecution. Others in this world suffer physically with illness. Difficult circumstances bring suffering. None of these things are easy to bear, and doubtless faith falters occasionally, but there is one thing which helps us to keep going in troubled times. It is the expectation of Heaven. Contemplating it **does** bring results. The Christian can say 'I know where I am going', and they do know. The Holy Spirit delights in bringing thoughts of Home to our minds, and He is very good at it. We do not minimise the pain of our trials and sufferings, but, if our attitude is right, they serve to make Heaven more real and desirable than ever. Paul knew plenty about suffering and testing, but he had his sights firmly set on his eternal future and he said – *For our light and momentary troubles are achieving for us an eternal glory that far outweighs them all* (2 Corinthians 4:17). He had things in a right context; his priorities were right. During a time of intense trial in my own life I was miserable and resentful. My cry was like that of many others – 'why should I have to suffer like this?' The Holy Spirit spoke to me saying 'put your sufferings up against those of Jesus on the Cross; then see if there is any comparison.' Of course there was no comparison. I found it then, and I still find it a very healthy exercise. Then He urged me to compare my troubles with the blessing of Heaven. Again, there was no comparison. I have valued that advice ever since.

It checks the spirit of the world

We have not received the **spirit of the world** *but the Spirit who is from God, that we may understand what God has freely given us* (1 Corinthians 2:12). The *spirit of the world* (mankind without God) seeks to satisfy the appetites of the flesh without restriction. 'The flesh' mentioned in the Bible means 'the seat of sin in mankind', or the lusts of our human nature, as in the following verse – *For they mouth empty, boastful words and, by appealing to the **lustful desires of sinful human nature**, they entice people who are just escaping from those who live in error* (2 Peter 2:18). *For everything in the world – **the cravings of sinful man**, the lust of his eyes and the boasting of what he has and does – comes not from the Father but from the world* (1 John 2:16). Sadly, even the Christian still has the flesh or old nature to contend with from time to time. So, we need all the help we can get. Contemplation of Heaven does make us more interested in the next life than the present one. It does help us to turn our thoughts away from the sinful urges of our body and mind. Our desires are not all bad. The sexual urge is God-given, but it is what we do with it that determines whether we fall into sin or not.

Contemplating Heaven does help us to avoid sin and temptation. We can help ourselves. We do have our part to play, for God will not do anything that we can do, although He will do everything that we cannot do. We can purify ourselves – *How can a young man keep his way pure? By living according to your word. I seek you with all my heart; do not let me stray from your commands. I have hidden your word in my heart that I might not sin against you* (Psalm 119:9–11). Why should God allow us to be slack and lazy? Those who truly love God will gladly do their part and co-operate with God.

Contemplating Hell brings results

It increases our gratitude to God

Thinking about it can increase our gratitude to God for saving us from its horrors. If you are a Christian why not thank Him now! It can increase our love for Him as we think about Him choosing us to be with Him forever, and not without Him forever. As we consider the terrible results of sin, it will surely help us to hate it all the more, and therefore to turn more quickly away from sinning. It can help us to respond to His deep desire for the salvation of souls so that we engage more earnestly in evangelism.

Jesus is an evangelist after all. It can help us to see the value of a soul to God in that He went to such lengths to save us from an awful destiny (see chapter 15 – 'Man's Value in God's Sight'). Man was made for eternity not time alone. God never wants mankind to miss their proper destiny. It can never be completely fulfilled on earth. It can never be fulfilled at all in Hell, but only in Heaven. All Christians are called to work together with God in this great work of saving mankind from Hell and transferring them to Heaven – *giving thanks to the Father, who has qualified you to share in the inheritance of the saints in the **kingdom of light**. For he has rescued us from the dominion of darkness and brought us into the kingdom of the Son he loves* (Colossians 1:12–13).

It increases our hatred of sin

As we see the results of sin in Hell, how loathsome it is to God, we must surely see sin from God's perspective. It is only right that we should see His perspective on it, and as we do so, turn from it more quickly than we do, and learn to hate it as Jesus did – *But about the Son he says, 'Your throne, O God, will last for ever and ever, and righteousness will be the sceptre of your kingdom. You have loved righteousness and hated wickedness'* (Hebrews 1:8–9).

It can reveal imbalance in our preaching

Many Christian leaders are guilty before God, because they either refrain from preaching about Heaven and Hell, or they are simply neglecting to preach about them. God never excuses sin in His people, especially leaders because they have greater responsibility. He expects us to deal with the sin of neglect. But He is so willing to help us do so because we are so precious to Him.

It can help us to be unselfish with the Gospel

Contemplating Hell should rebuke all who are selfish with it. Remember the fearful warning to cowardly Christians – *When I say to the wicked, 'O wicked man, you will surely die,' and you do not speak out to dissuade him from his ways, that wicked man will die for his sin, and I will hold you accountable for his blood* (Ezekiel 33:8).

It increases our compassion for the lost

Compassion is a lovely word. It means sympathy, mercy, feeling the pain of others, and reaching out to them. God showed it to Israel – *In all their distress he too was distressed, and the angel of his presence saved them. In his love and mercy he redeemed them; he lifted them up and carried them all the days of old* (Isaiah 63:9). Jesus showed it when He was on earth – *Jesus had compassion on them and touched their eyes. Immediately they received their sight and followed him* (Matthew 20:34). Reading about Hell will help us to do the same.

It urges us on to mission and evangelism

Our gratitude to God for our deliverance should cause us to reach out to the other people whom God wants to be with Him in Heaven. If we don't do so, we are not really grateful. We can say that we are, but words can be cheap. It is possible for Christians to be very selfish about Heaven. It is wholly right to be constantly thinking about it, but if we never tell unbelievers about the joy and glory of Heaven, then we are selfish, and guilty of the crime of silence. There is indeed a Heaven to be gained, but there is also a Hell to be shunned. Both must be spoken about to the world.

If we are rejoicing in the privilege of going to Heaven it should spill over in our conversation with our neighbours. We have good news to share. We should share it, bubbling over with enthusiasm as we speak about it. We also have bad news to share, and we must ask God for the grace to share it, and the courage to tell the whole truth about it.

The reason for this book is to help us to see the sheer contrast between our eternal future and that of the unsaved, and be stimulated by it to reach out to the lost. Remember the value of a soul.

It urges us on to intercession

Although I have written about the real terrors of Hell – God's anger, judgement, and punishment – there are people alive now who could yet be saved from it by repentance. But it will only come about through our preaching and our intercession. God wants more intercessors – *I looked for a man among them who would build up the wall and stand before me in the gap on behalf of the land so I would not have to destroy it, but I found none* (Ezekiel 22:30). Those who stood in the gap and built the walls were those who fulfilled a vital role, essential for the safety of others. If God cannot find enough intercessors to open the way for the Gospel to those who have not heard it yet, could it be your fault? Moses was an intercessor. He heard God say after Israel sinned yet again – *'Now leave me alone so that my anger may burn against them and that I may destroy them. Then I will make you into a great nation.'* But Moses (did not leave it there, he) *sought the favour of the LORD his God. 'O LORD,'* he said, *'why should your anger burn against your people, whom you brought out of Egypt with great power and a mighty hand? Why should the Egyptians say, "It was with evil intent that he brought them out, to kill them in the mountains and to wipe them off the face of the earth"? Turn from your fierce anger; relent and do not bring disaster on your people'* (Exodus 32:10–12). How essential the prayers of Moses were for the nation in deadly danger. The Psalm says about God – *So he said he would destroy them – had not Moses, his chosen one, stood in the breach before him to keep his wrath from destroying them* (Psalm 106:23).

It focuses the need for missionaries

In other words – Gospel preachers. All those who have been transferred from darkness to light, i.e. Christians, can be missionaries. The term simply means those who go some-where with a message. Those who go abroad are fewer these days, but everyone can go somewhere with the great-est message in the world. Including you!

Having read this book, what shall we do now? Action is surely called for! Or shall we just brush aside these truths. Having written about the value of thinking about Heaven, I want to stress that there is also a value in thinking about Hell. No one really wants to think about Hell for very long, and in fact very few preachers preach about it because it is a horrible subject. And yet, Jesus preached about it! So, because of the need of the heathen, both civilised and un-civilised, to hear the Gospel, shall we join the intercessors, and the missionaries? Shall we get on with God in the great task of changing this world in preparation for the perfec-tion of the next? But we will never do it alone. We need help. Praise God that we can have the help of the Holy Spirit. When He sees us starting to contemplate Heaven, and to speak about it to one another, He will help us to 'Turn our eyes upon Jesus ... and the things of earth will grow strangely dim in the light of His glory and grace'. He knows that when we meditate on Jesus, and turn our thoughts to Heaven, this world grows dim, and that world grows bright! Similarly, when He sees us make the first move in contemplating Hell, and therefore reaching out to the lost with the Gospel, He will come quickly to our aid. He will not necessarily make it easy, but He will make it possible. He will remind us of the urgency in the heart of Jesus when He said – *I have **other** sheep ... I must bring them also. They too will listen to my voice, and there shall be one flock and one shepherd* (John 10:16). Note the urgency in Jesus' voice in this verse. *I must bring others.* I expect His desire is to bring them **to** Heaven, and save them **from** Hell. Shall we rise up and get on with this work – with Him? God bless you as you do so.

Appendix 1

The Millenium

I have no space to go into great detail about the Millenium. We should understand that the Bible does not give us a watertight understanding of eschatology, so, we must be careful of too much dogmatism. There are several views concerning the Millenium, and I give a very brief summary of most of their beliefs below.

A-Millenialism

Some A-Millenialists disagree with the following in some of the details. They emphasise what the Millenium is **not**!

They say that God rules **now**, not then. There is therefore no earthly reign of Christ. Prophecies are fulfilled within the history of the church, not within the 1000 years reign. The Second Coming inaugurates the final age, and state of saved and unsaved. The two Resurrections occur together – no 1000 year reign in between. They say 1000 Years is symbolic = perfection.

Some A-Millenialists believe the Gospel will reach all the world and the church will dominate it. Other A-Millenialists are more pessimistic – like Pre-Millenialists. Christ's Coming is imminent – there are no events required before it.

Post-Millenialism

Some Post Millenialists disagree with the following in some of the details.

They believe that the Church is militant and triumphant in this age. The Kingdom is established now, i.e. prior to the Return.

Social transformation. We should be involved in poverty, injustice etc. Christ's Return is dependent on **all** hearing the Gospel. It cannot occur until the Tribulation (happening now) is completed. They expect mass revival. The world is being Christianised. There will be a brief apostasy. There will be the Advent, Resurrection, and Final Judgement.

Israel is not seen as distinct. Some Post-Millenialists say that if the salvation of Israel plus release of salvation for Gentiles precedes the Return, then Jewish evangelism is important now.

Pre-Millenialism

Some Pre-Millenialists disagree with the following in some of the details.

These tend to be pre-tribulationalists, i.e. the saints both dead and alive are raptured or resurrected before the Tribulation. No prophecies remain to be fulfilled first before His Coming. Only a remnant will be saved. So let us get as many saved as possible now. They tend to keep clear of politics etc. Most say that the Age of miracles is over. They believe in a literal 1000 year reign with Jesus on earth, during which He reigns with unlimited power. This reign will be inaugurated with a cataclysm. Satan is bound for the period then destroyed. There will be universal peace and harmony in all Creation (Romans 8).

All this is preceded by the great Tribulation (Luke 2:21–33), during which there will be wars, moral decay, and natural disasters. In their view the Return is imminent. Many Pre-Millenialists believe that Israel has special status.

A personal view

Those who write books should declare where they stand, so

I will say that I believe in a modified form of Pre-Millenialism. I grew up believing in a fairly extreme form of this doctrine, and I accepted it uncritically until I started preaching it. Then I had to work out what was my own belief, and that which I had accepted simply because my church elders taught it.

I believe that Jesus will reign on the renewed earth and that I will reign with Him. I am not sure as to the actual duration of it, but I see no reason to reject the 1000 year period mentioned in Revelation – *Blessed and holy are those who have part in the first resurrection. The second death has no power over them, but they will be priests of God and of Christ and will reign with him for **a thousand years*** (Revelation 20:6).

I cannot see that we will escape the Tribulation, but I believe that Tribulation grace will be given to us when we need it. God promised it to us – *But he said to me, 'My grace is sufficient for you, for my power is made perfect in weakness.' Therefore I will boast all the more gladly about my weaknesses, so that Christ's power may rest on me* (2 Corinthians 12:9). After all, what can separate us from the resources of God? The Bible says again – *Who shall separate us from the love of Christ? Shall trouble or hardship or persecution or famine or nakedness or danger or sword?* (Romans 8:35).

I believe that God still has special purposes for Israel. I love the nation, and have preached there and prayed for the nation for many years. But I am not one of those ardent pro-Israel Christians who cannot believe that Israel can ever be wrong. In addition I believe that the Jewish people need the same Gospel that Gentiles need, and are just as much sinners in God's sight as we are.

I believe that there will be a great Revival before Jesus comes again. I have prayed for it for nearly 50 years, and hope I see it before I die. I thank God for the great outpouring of His Spirit that we are seeing today, but it is not Revival.

The main thing

I believe that eschatology is important, and that the church today, generally speaking, is deficient in understanding these things. However, I feel that we should get on with preaching the Gospel more than worrying over too many details in eschatology. The main thing is that Jesus will return in glory, and we should be ready to greet Him with joy and not with shame.

Appendix 2

Cry of the Blood

One of the things which profoundly affected me in my early Christian days was the following tract. It caused me to put fear and shyness aside, to knock on doors, and to urge people to be saved.

Cry *of the Blood*

The tom toms thumped on all night, and the darkness shuddered around me like a living, feeling thing. I could not go to sleep, so I lay awake and looked; and I saw, and it seemed like this:

That I stood on a grassy sward, and at my feet a precipice broke sheer down into infinite space. I looked, but saw no bottom; only cloud shapes, black and furiously coiled, and great shadow-shrouded hollows, and unfathomable depths. Back I drew, dizzy at the depth.

Then I saw forms of people moving single file along the grass. They were making for the edge. There was a woman with a baby in her arms and another little child holding on to her dress. She was on the very verge. Then I saw that she was blind. She lifted her foot for the next step – it trod air. She was over, and the children went over with her. Oh, the cry as they went over!

Then I saw more streams of people flowing from all quarters. All were blind, stone blind; all made straight for the precipice edge. There were shrieks as they suddenly knew themselves falling, and a tossing up of helpless arms, catching, clutching at empty air. But some went over quietly and fell without a sound.

Then I wondered, with a wonder that was simply agony, why no one stopped them at the edge. I could not. I was glued to the ground, and I could not call. Though I strained and tried, only a whisper would come.

Then I saw that at the edge there were sentries set at intervals. But the intervals were far too great; there were wide, unguarded gaps between. And over these gaps the people feel in their blindness, quite unwarned; and the green grass seemed blood red to me, and the gulf yawned like the mouth of Hell.

Then I saw, like the pictures of peace, a group of people under some trees, with their backs turned towards the gulf. They were making daisy chains. Sometimes, when a piercing shriek cut the quiet air and reached them, it disturbed them and they thought it rather a vulgar noise. And if one of their number started up and wanted to go and do something to help, then all the others would pull that one down. 'Why should you get so excited about it? You must wait for a definite "call" to go. You haven't finished your daisy chains. It would be really selfish' they said 'to leave us to finish the work alone.'

There was another group. It was made up of people whose great desire was to get some sentries out; but they found that very few wanted to go, and sometimes there were no sentries for miles and miles at the edge.

Once a girl stood alone in her place, waving the people back; but her mother and the other relations called, and reminded her that her furlough was due; she must not break the 'rules'. And, being tired and needing a change, she had to go and rest awhile; but no one was sent to guard her gap, and over and over the people fell, like a waterfall of souls.

Once a child caught at a tuft of grass that grew on the very brink of the gulf; the child clung convulsively, and it called but nobody seemed to hear. And the little girl who longed to be back in her gap thought she heard the little one cry, and she sprang up and wanted to go; at which her relatives reproved her, reminding her that no one is necessary anywhere – the gap would be well taken care of, they knew. And they sang a hymn.

Then through the hymn came another sound like the pain of a million broken hearts wrung out in one full drop, one sob. And a horror of great darkness was upon **me**, for I knew what it was – the cry of the blood.

Then I heard the voice of the Lord saying, 'Whom shall I send? And who will go for us?' And I said, 'Here am I. Send me!' He said, 'Go and tell this people: "Be ever hearing, but never understanding; be ever seeing, but never perceiving."' (Isaiah 6:8–9 NIV). *He said to them, 'Go into all the world and preach the good news to all creation'* (Mark 16:15 NIV), *and teaching them to obey everything I have commanded you. And surely I am with you always, to the very end of the age* (Matthew 28:20 NIV).

Amy Carmichael

Appendix 3

Arguments against the Doctrine of Hell

Annihilation

This is the argument that when we die we cease to exist. The Bible does not support this at all – *and the dust returns to the ground it came from, and the **spirit returns to God** who gave it* (Ecclesiastes 12:7). Man's spirit does not cease to exist. A further proof is the verse – *Then they will go away to **eternal** punishment, but the righteous to **eternal** life* (Matthew 25:46). They go to an eternal state, not into annihilation. Yet another proof is the verse – *And the smoke of their torment rises for **ever and ever**. There is no rest day or night for those who worship the beast and his image, or for anyone who receives the mark of his name* (Revelation 14:11). *For ever and ever*; the phrase 'ever and ever' contradicts the idea of annihilation. The second death is no more a cessation of being than the first death. It is an eternal awareness of God's anger and displeasure. Annihilationalism is a view which seeks to avoid the concept of punishment. I do not believe this view at all.

Soul sleep

This is the idea that people go into a kind of trance after death, so that they are not conscious and cannot therefore be in pain, trouble, or under judgement. It is an unscriptural heresy – the Bible says nothing at all about soul sleep. In fact, Jesus tells of the **conscious** experience of the rich man after he died. How can he be conscious if he is asleep? (The event is recorded in Luke chapter 16.) Those who are saved when they die are 'asleep' in the sense that they are unaware as far as life on earth is concerned, but they cannot be unconscious or asleep. How could they be with God around! The Psalmist expected to be very much awake in the presence of God – *And I – in righteousness I will* ***see your face; when I awake***, *I will be satisfied with seeing your likeness* (Psalm 17:15). He expected to be consciously rejoicing too – *You have made known to me the path of life; you will fill me with* ***joy in your presence***, *with eternal pleasures at your right hand* (Psalms 16:11). John the Apostle saw very clearly that we would be wide awake – *They will see his face, and his name will be on their foreheads* (Revelation 22:4). Critics of the Bible use the following verse to bolster their belief that after death we know nothing because we 'sleep' – *For the living know that they will die, but the dead know nothing; they have no further reward, and even the memory of them is forgotten* (Ecclesiastes 9:5). But alongside this verse, we must put the verses above, otherwise we fall into error as those who believe in soul sleep have done.

I write about the consciousness of the unsaved in chapter 19 – 'Death and Resurrection for the Lost' in the section on Hell.

There is no devil

This is nonsense for several reasons – one is that Jesus refers to him many times. He says in the Bible – *and the enemy who sows them is the devil. The harvest is the end of the age, and the harvesters are angels* (Matthew 13:39). *Then he will say to those on his left, 'Depart from me, you who are cursed, into the eternal fire prepared for the devil and his angels'* (Matthew 25:41). *You belong to your father, the devil, and you want to carry out your father's desire. He was a murderer from the beginning, not holding to the truth, for there is no truth in him. When he lies, he speaks his native language, for he is a liar and the father of lies* (John 8:44).

Secondly, any Christian knows that the devil is real. We are – ...*not unaware of his schemes* (2 Corinthians 2:11). Every day we are tempted, hindered, and assailed by a being who is a liar, murderer, and a tempter. Praise God that temptation is not sin, for Jesus was tempted, but He never sinned, neither need we!

Thirdly, evil in the world is not a haphazard erupting of evil – it is co-ordinated. This necessitates a co-ordinator. The Bible says that this person is the devil, who is an intelligent being. All the evil powers mentioned in Scripture are under his control, and they serve him – *For our struggle is not against flesh and blood, but against the rulers, against the authorities, against the powers of this dark world and against the spiritual forces of evil in the heavenly realms* (Ephesians 6:12). The devil uses deadly weapons such as fear, murder, sexual perversion, and lies. Such things did not just evolve, they were thought out by an evil intelligent being – Satan.

Evil is relative

The atheists and humanists who believe this idea say that there is no law which points out the difference between good and evil, there fore we define it ourselves according to our own code of practice. But Christians say that God's Law defines what is evil and what is good. His Laws are given as a blessing and a safeguard. Man cannot alter His Laws, and they ignore them at their peril, for God says that all transgression of His Law is sin. Obedience to the whole Law is required, and this is impossible apart from the power which is given to the saved – *For whoever keeps the whole law and yet stumbles at just one point is guilty of breaking all of it* (James 2:10). Jesus preached the Law, but He gave us a different motive for obeying it. Whereas the Israelites had to obey it or else! Christians respond to Jesus' word – *If you love me, you will obey what I command* (John 14:15).

A loving God could not throw people into such a place

Admittedly the Bible seems to indicate that God throws them into Hell – *But I will show you whom you should fear: Fear him who, after the killing of the body, has power to **throw you into hell**. Yes, I tell you, fear him* (Luke 12:5). But He does not just throw people into Hell **against their will**. The picture of an angry God grabbing struggling sinners and throwing them vengefully into the flames originated with the cartoonists, not with the Bible. God simply confirms the choice that people made before they died, and He than assigns them to the place which **they** have chosen. God gave us freewill, and we all use it to make a decision as to where we will spend eternity. When we have done so, God confirms our decision – *Let him who does wrong continue to do wrong; let him who is vile continue to be vile; let him who does right continue to do right; and let him who is holy continue to be holy* (Revelation 22:11).

Hell is only our 'cross' or suffering on earth

The Bible says that Judgement and Hell comes **after** death not before it – *Just as man is destined to die once, and after that to face judgment* (Hebrews 9:27). The Bible also says that Hell is an **eternal** condition, not one that we can experience on earth.

Hell simply means death, or grave

'Thanatos' is the Greek word meaning 'death'; i.e. the separation of the soul and the body. It is not interchangeable with the word Hell. It does not mean the same thing. The soul never dies. *'Mnemeion'* is the Greek word for 'grave' – a place where a dead body is buried. It cannot have the meaning of Hell or anything like it.